<u>The</u> *Ultimate* <u>**Horse and Rider Partnership**</u>

Natural Western Riding

The *Ultimate* Horse and Rider Partnership

Natural Western Riding

Don Blazer/Cathy Hanson

Revised Edition
Editing by Meribah Small
Cover design by Janie White
Trail Courses by Cherie Vonada
Photographs by Sonja Allmendinger
Riding demonstrations by Cathy Hanson

www.donblazer.com
Success Is Easy, Scottsdale, AZ

Published by **Success Is Easy**
13610 N. Scottsdale Rd.
Suite 10-406
Scottsdale, AZ 85254

First published as a Success Is Easy paperback in 2001

Library of Congress Control Number 01-126054

ISBN 0-9660127-4-7

Printed in the United States of America

For Rick and Taylor
with love

Cathy

Thanks to the horses

Table of Contents

Introduction

In the original "Introduction" to this book, written many years ago, I said we were moving away from the art of authentic western riding. At that time I wasn't sure if it was because we failed to remember its purpose, or as we became more sophisticated, we were embarrassed by its short history. Maybe we were simply trying to improve our horsemanship by moving toward the classic style of riding, or maybe it was an effort to gain greater acceptance from horsemen in general.

Fortunately, today we are remembering the purpose of western riding, and we are no longer embarrassed by our roots. We have gained a new pride in our past and we are confident of our knowledge and skills. Western riders have proven themselves the equal of any horseman.

Western riders have transcended all other styles of riding in the creation of harmony and equality between horse and rider. Western riders are the only riders bold enough, brave enough, confident enough to request an action, then allow the horse total freedom to release all his brilliance and magic. Today it is all other styles of riding which should look to western riders for inspiration and direction.

Still, we must be careful, for in today's world of specialization we are exaggerating and distorting performances until they violate all the principles of a true partnership. In some competitive events, we are moving ever closer to domination of and surrender by our horses. We must keep our focus on the truth of western riding, constantly examining our direction and always challenging our skills.

True western riding was created by the American cowboy who lived it and survived because of it, and in his work made it an almost flawless art.

The American cowboy was a peon, a laborer, a drifter who did not rely on knowledge of anatomy, equine or otherwise, to control the horse. He did not apply the techniques of dressage or any other scientific interpretation of correct aids to instruct his horse. He had neither the desire nor the time to practice horsemanship for its beauty nor to pursue its perfection for pure pleasure.

The American cowboy did not adopt the European horseman's idea of man's superiority and the horse's inferiority. He knew his life, his spirit, was never separate from his horse.

Out of necessity and the recognition of his own limitations, and an appreciation for his horse's unique talents, the cowboy formed a true partnership with his companion. He made the decision as to what work was to be done and then he requested the help of his partner. And once having asked, he extended his reins, giving freedom to his partner, allowing the horse to work on his own. The horse, for the first time, was no longer a servant, but a part of the oneness which exists when man accepts the nature of his universe.

Unfortunately, the idea of encouraging the partnership between man and horse as the purpose of western riding is still ignored when riders are instructed to use a balanced seat and the upright equitation position of stylized movements. The advice offered does not make better riders. It simply produces western riders who conform to exploited images of greater and greater specialization. Certainly the riders don't lack talent. They are merely willing to accept a lower level of perfection in return for a blue ribbon. There is no glory in dulling the performance of the horse to elicit a boring but technically flawless trip around a show ring rail.

Constant control and domination of a horse always results in the sublimation of his talents. Under the expensive, heavily merchandised facade, the horse's energy waits to be freed once again. The horse may have been trained into submissiveness, but his fire can be rekindled.

And the awakening has occurred worldwide, and the concept of equality of horse and rider is now the standard by which all riders and riding is measured.

This truth of western riding is expanding, washing away the "control" mentality of other styles. We see it most often in the competitions of cowboys at work--cutting, roping, working cow horse. But we now also see it in the trail class, stadium jumping and the cross-country portion of three-day eventing. The style and freedom of a true man-horse partnership is gaining momentum and the philosophy of it will sweep over all forms of horsemanship.

This book is for those who wish to understand and experience an equal partnership between man and horse. It is for those who wish to feel the exhilaration and joyous harmony of oneness.

It is for those who would give rather than take. It is for the western rider.

Only freedom and giving can take you to your dreams.

1

Taking a Natural Seat

Western riding is not classical dressage, nor park seat, nor hunt seat. It was never intended to be.

Western riding began as an adaptation to need, just as all riding styles have done. In the case of western riding, it was the need of the working cowboy to use his horse to herd cattle, to move with great flexibility and, at times, with speed. To do this to perfection, the horse needed complete freedom.

This freedom runs counter to the classic style of horsemanship, in which the rider dictates all the horse's movements by giving subtle, controlled cues and receiving subtle, controlled responses, if the horse is well disciplined.

The western rider must likewise ask for a response by giving a subtle cue, but then must relinquish control, leaving the movement of the horse to the horse, a willing, free spirit.

The results of the two styles are as different as the concepts, and correctly so.

Both styles represent skill and patience and ultimately the achievement of the desired response.

Neither style can claim to be better than the other, and neither is more important nor more valuable. If honestly practiced, each style gives its own reward. But it is only in western riding that the unbridled brilliance of the horse is allowed to shine singularly. Only in western riding are the talents of the horse and horseman appreciated equally. Western riders never applaud a disciplined performance in response to a dominating rider.

Giving complete freedom to the horse is the principal difference between the classic style of riding and western riding. To give that freedom, the western rider must abandon the classical rider's goal of always being in the center of his horse. Staying at the center point of a "free" western horse at work is an impossibility. The horse's action is simply too fast. Attempting to remain in the center of the horse becomes an interference and dulls the performance.

The rider of a responsive western horse must anticipate and lead the horse with a weight-shift cue. If in turning to the right, the rider turns her body and looks to the right, she leads the horse, and the responsive horse moves under the rider's weight, bringing them back into balance.

If the rider asks for a response from the horse, then attempts to remain in the center of the horse, she will undoubtedly find herself behind the horse's movement. The rider cannot catch up with the natural action of the western horse unless she restricts that action, slowing it to a pace at which the rider can function. To do so is a violation of the principle of the request-response partnership. The western horse which is working correctly can perform better on his own. The astute western rider

Turning her upper body, the rider shifts her weight to the left, leading the horse to the left. The horse moves left to pick up the rider's weight and bring the partnership back into balance.

will let him do so, interfering as little as possible with the horse's natural talent.

The western rider, to facilitate freedom for the horse, takes a natural seat.

Mounting should be done in a relaxed, practical and safe manner. The rider may mount from either side; neither is preferred. Mounting alternately from side to side keeps the stirrup leathers stretched equally.

The reins, of equal length on each side of the horse's neck, if taken in the left hand should be shortened to the point of light mouth contact. The horse's head should remain straight forward, or turned very slightly to the left. If mounting on the right side, the reins are taken in the right hand and the horse's nose is tipped slightly to the right.

Once the reins are positioned, the rider should turn her body so she is facing in the same direction as the horse. If mounting on the left, the left foot is positioned in the stirrup, and with the left hand on the horse's neck and the right hand on the saddle horn, the rider lifts her body by straightening her left leg. The rider remains facing forward, always looking in the same direction as the horse, and never allowing her body to turn toward the saddle. The rider should never attempt to pull herself up with her arms, but should always rise by using the strength in her leg.

The rider's hands help hold the upper body steady and in the forward facing position.

The rider's right leg is allowed to move slightly back toward the horse's hindquarters and is then swung over the horse's rump and to the horse's right side. The rider sits gently in the saddle. The rider does not look down to find the right stirrup, but locates it and positions her foot by feel.

Dismounting is the same procedure in reverse.

Once seated, the rider should be able to keep her heels lower than her toes easily by simply extending the calf muscles of her legs.

The rider's body is erect, yet relaxed, and the rider does not, as so many advocate, attempt to push her shoulders back, hold her chin rigidly up, or keep the back of the heels against an imaginary line running down her arched back.

The rider should sit down on the horse as if she had been lowered into place from a point of suspension above the horse. The rider will take a deep seat, with legs extended directly below the body, the natural position of sitting toward the front and inside of the thighs. The shoulders will be relaxed, but not allowed to curl forward. The rider keeps her chin up in order to look ahead and focus on the direction of travel.

Each rider, as each horse, is an individual. Taking a natural seat on one horse will not be the same as taking a natural seat on another. What one rider considers a natural seat will not be the same as it is for another. The physical forms of horses and riders dictate the natural seat which is never rigid, restrictive or an interference to the horse.

Riding principles remain constant, but their application should never be forced. Straining to reach an artificial position in the saddle is never the best choice.

By taking a natural seat, the rider finds she automatically sits as close to the horse as is

Taking a natural seat, the rider finds it takes no conscious effort to sit deep in the saddle and close to the horse. It's natural.

possible when a saddle is used. Even with the large western saddle, the natural-seat rider will discover she is able to feel the horse's movements easily, and with practice, can soon anticipate the horse's intended movement.

By sitting naturally on the horse, making no special effort to establish an artificially correct position, the rider finds it requires no strain on her part to maintain her own natural body carriage.

And as the rider gains confidence, she discovers it is not necessary to grip with the knees to stay with the horse. Instead, it is much to her advantage to remain relaxed, in a position to maintain light contact with her lower leg.

Also, by sitting naturally, the rider sits straight down on the horse. This makes the major contact point the front portion of the inner thighs rather than the buttocks. The rider's legs are then essentially positioned below the torso.

The rider sits straight down on the inner part of the thigh.

The rider must now establish the closeness of leg contact which is necessary to the subtle control of the horse as well as giving the rider a secure seat. Her secure seat results from the depth of the seat, not from gripping with the thighs. The rider should allow the upper legs to relax, while the lower legs are gently placed against the horse's sides. To achieve this deep seat and close contact, the rider must keep her heels lower than her toes. To do this, she must extend the calf muscles of the legs. This is difficult for the beginning rider, for the muscles must be conditioned. With practice, however, it becomes effortless.

Once the rider is seated on the front part of the inner thighs, with her heels lower than her toes, she finds she is "with the horse", sensitive to the horse's movements, in balance and secure.

Heels lower than toes, yet no weight is placed in stirrup.

By sitting deep in the saddle, the rider allows her body weight to be carried by the saddle seat. The rider does not put body weight in the stirrups. The stirrups are held in place by pressure which originates from the extension of the calf muscles when the heel is dropped lower than the toe. This pressure has nothing to do with the rider's body weight. The western rider can sample such pressure by sitting in a chair, lifting the feet off the floor, and extending the calf muscles. The pressure created can be felt in the balls of the feet, yet it is obvious there is no body weight on the feet.

The rider must not attempt to grip the horse with her knees, as this requires a tensing of the torso muscles, which immediately reduces the suppleness of the rider's body. Once suppleness of the upper body is lost, there is a corresponding increase in the weight of the upper body, making the rider top-heavy. The top-heavy western rider is almost always behind the movement of her horse, an unacceptable position.

The rider's elbows should be relaxed. The elbows should be at the rider's sides, but not consciously held close to the body. The good western rider will move her elbows forward and back to change the length of the rein or to lead the horse into movement. Restricting elbow movement is contrary to the free flow of the natural seat and flexibility of the rider's upper body. Wildly flopping elbows extending well out from the rider's sides are never acceptable.

The rider should never fear changing the rein in the hand if not doing so restricts or forces a static position of the elbow. If the elbow is held stationary, the result is that the horse eventually hits the bit or is unduly bumped by the bit. Holding the elbows in a fixed position also causes the rider to tense her back muscles, thereby reducing flexibility which is detrimental to the natural seat.

Western reins, which may be held in either hand, are grasped in one of two styles. The Texas style, used in the majority of states, requires the use of split reins. The rider accepts the reins by placing them across the upturned palm of her right hand. The right thumb and index finger then grasp the reins, and the hand is then rolled toward the left, bringing the thumb and index finger to the top. The wrist is held

Texas style--split reins--held in the rider's right hand.

straight. There should be no up, down, forward or backward slant to the hand.

The hand may be held just in front of and below the saddle horn, or it may be held slightly above the saddle horn. When held in front of the saddle horn, there is a natural twist to the rider's shoulder which results in one shoulder leading the other. If the hand is held above the saddle horn, there is almost always an upward tilt to the forearm.

The hand may be held above or below the saddle horn.

The idle hand does not touch the reins when the Texas style is used, and is held either at the rider's waist or, as I prefer, down at the left thigh.

With the California, or old Spanish style of reining, the rider accepts the reins by placing the palm of her left hand down upon the reins, then grasping them in the thumb and index finger and rolling the hand away from the body so the thumb and index finger are up. For California reining, the reins are closed and a romal is attached. The romal is held in the right hand, which is carried on the right thigh. Just how far down the romal the rider wants to put her right hand depends on what is most comfortable under the circumstances. (Some association show rules prescribe a minimum distance between the hands. Check the rule book.)

In California-style reining, the reining hand is also held in front of, or just above the saddle horn. The decision is with the rider. No matter the choice of reining style, the rider should keep the reins as low as is comfortable. A low hand has an influence on the horse's head carriage. A horse which carries his head low will have more quickness in his turns.

California style allows no fingers between the reins.

The rider must use her fingers, not her entire hand, when moving the reins to cue or control the horse. Since the rider has grasped the reins between the thumb and index finger, the remaining three fingers are free to play upon the reins. The rider should spread these fingers to a degree, thereby allowing herself the opportunity to shorten, lengthen or bump the reins with the fingers without the necessity of moving the whole hand or arm.

Rolling the wrist in the desired direction of travel is all that should be required to neck-rein the highly polished western horse. Movement of the entire arm may be necessary with the green or even the intermediate horse in order to evoke the correct response. Even under these circumstances, the rider will find the free movement of the fingers is an added advantage.

If it is necessary to shorten or lengthen the reins to a greater degree than can be accomplished through the contraction or relaxation of the fingers, then the rider has the option of twisting the wrist away, or toward her body or moving her elbow.

Gripping the reins with only the thumb and index finger helps the rider keep her hands light. And as I will repeat often, light (good) hands are possessed only by the rider who make full use of leg cues.

Bosal or snaffle reins, for training, are held in two hands.

The rider should not look down unnecessarily, but should always try to be looking in the direction or intended direction of travel. Looking down brings the upper body forward, and while it might make only the slightest degree of change, the sensitive horse will respond, generally by an increase in speed. Do not stare at the horse's head; this too causes the upper body to lean forward.

A deep seat helps keep the rider's legs directly under the body and the rider's spine in alignment with horse's spine.

Most often a rider is tempted to look down for one of two reasons. First, the rider is trying to determine on which lead the horse is working. Second, the rider is trying to locate a stirrup. There is no good excuse for either. The good western rider determines the horse's lead by feel, as I will explain later. The good western rider also knows, through practice and feel, the location of the stirrup.

The best stirrup length for the natural-seat rider is determined by having the rider sit on the horse with her legs relaxed and hanging at full length. The bottom of the stirrups should be just below the rider's ankle. In this position, the rider need only lift her toes in order to put her feet in the stirrups.

As the feet are inserted in the stirrups, the rider should rest them against the inside edge of the stirrups. The pressure against the stirrups should be applied by the balls of the feet. If the rider has lifted her toes in order to place her feet in the stirrups, she will find her toes are somewhat higher than the heels and the calf muscles of the legs are stretched properly.

Adjusted correctly, the stirrup length will allow the western rider to position her legs almost directly under her body. The legs are correctly positioned if the rider can, without leaning forward, look down and see just the tips of her toes. If her knee blocks her view of her toes, then the stirrups are too short and the leg has too much bend. If she can see past her knee, and see most of her foot, then her leg is too straight and pulled too far rearward.

If necessary to achieve proper leg position, the rider must punch new holes in the stirrup leathers.

As ridiculous as it may seem to the serious student, too many riders simply adjust the stirrups to the saddle maker's predetermined lengths, whether correct or not. A good rider will always make the necessary adjustments to keep the stirrup leathers even. Over a period of time, the left stirrup leather stretches from the extra stain encountered when the rider constantly mounts and dismounts on the left side. A good western horse will accept a rider mounting and dismounting from either side. And there are plenty of good reasons for a working western rider to mount from either side. Use both sides equally.

Having the stirrups at the correct length helps achieve the natural closeness of the rider's body to the horse. This closeness helps the rider to sit deep and remain balanced in turns or in the center of the horse when that position is desired.

When the rider sits in the center of the horse, the rider's spine and the horse's spin are aligned. This is correct when the western horse is at rest or is moving straight forward or straight back. However, the western rider will turn her upper body into the direction of travel when making a turn, and her spine will then be inclined toward the direction of travel. The rider must not lean too much into the turn, but should turn the upper body slightly shifting her weight into the turn and thereby leading the horse into the turn. When responding correctly, the western horse will follow the rider's lead, turning as requested and keeping the partnership in balance.

Shifting weight to the inside and leading the horse into a turn is correct when there is no lateral movement involved.

If the rider is sitting properly on the inside front portion of the thighs, the rider's tailbone will not come against the cantle of the saddle, not even when she leans a little backward and to the inside of a turn, a weight-shift position used in rollbacks and pivots on the hindquarters.

When remaining seated in the natural position, the rider finds that when the upper body is inclined in the direction of travel, her legs automatically and naturally move into the proper aid positions. If the turn is to the left, for example, the rider turns her upper body to the left, her left hip moves back, her right hip forward. The rider's legs move with the hips, the left leg moving back and the right leg moving forward. The legs take the natural position for assisting the horse in the turn. The left leg holds the hindquarters, allowing the horse to arc around the left leg. The right leg is forward to push the horse into a gradual or tight turn.

The natural seat is a relaxed seat. By sitting the natural seat, the western rider can function in harmony with the horse. Force, restrictive stiffness and artificial standards can be forgotten forever.

2

Tack--Choice, Use and Goals

The choice of saddle is important in riding the natural western seat. An equitation saddle will not do, nor will a cutting saddle nor a game saddle. Because form follows function in the design of all equipment, including the western saddle, it is obvious that before selection of a saddle, the rider must decide how the saddle is to be used.

For the western rider who wants to establish a partnership with his horse in performing fast exercises, the ranch saddle and the roper saddle are most acceptable. All other designs are too specialized and inhibit, rather than enhance, the natural western seat.

The equitation saddle is heavily padded in the seat between the swell and the cantle. This padding locks the rider down in the seat, giving her the feeling of being securely set in the proper position. However, when it comes time to work the horse or to free the horse for work with speed, the rider discovers she is still locked into position, unable to lead, and hardly able to follow the movements of the horse.

Today's cutting saddle and game saddle are designed exclusively for specific activities. Years ago, cutting was practiced by the cowboys who used an all-purpose ranch saddle. But now the art of cutting is generally reserved for the professional trainer or dedicated amateur who demand special assistance from their saddles.

Game saddles are for barrel racers and pole benders. They are cut small and are light, but they lack comfort and sufficient seat size for the working rider.

The roper saddle is functional enough for the natrual-seat rider, but its design does create some limitations. A good roper must stand in the stirrups to be in the proper position to catch a steer or calf. Therefore, there is little forward swing to the fenders, which are rather stiff. This rigidity keeps the roper from flopping back to the cantle when shifting to a standing position. Even though there is some restriction to the leg movement with the roper saddle, there is still sufficient freedom for the natural-seat rider to lead the horse.

The ranch saddle remains the best saddle for the rider who wants to flow with the movement of the horse. It has a more flexible fender, allowing greater freedom of leg movement. The seat is more or less in the center of the saddle, with virtually the same slope from the swell as from the cantle, so the rider is pushed neither forward nor back.

Unfortunately, by its style and design, the western saddle does keep the rider a fair distance from the horse, but this disadvantage can be minimized if the saddle fits the horse properly. The best saddle in either the roper or ranch type is the one in which the seat is narrow so the rider can easily keep her legs against the horse's sides.

A well-fitting saddle will have sufficient width at the gullet to fit over the horse's withers without applying painful pressure.

The twist of the saddle tree determines how the saddle fits the horse's back. If the bars of the saddle are the same in the back as at the gullet, the saddle may fit the withers, but it will be resting on top of the horse's back at the rear. A properly twisted tree will leave the bars narrow at the withers, but flat and wide at the rear of the saddle.

A relatively easy and safe test of a saddle fit can be made by saddling the horse with a single saddle pad, saddle blanket, and saddle. The horse should be worked until he is warm enough to produce some sweat under the saddle. If the saddle fits properly, when it is removed the sweat on the horse's back will be evenly distributed. If there are dry spots or spots which are excessively wet, then the saddle does not fit well.

In some cases, and ill-fitting saddle can be helped with extra padding. This solution will protect the horse until a well-fitting saddle can be obtained. The extra padding, however, does present the rider with another disadvantage. The heavy padding lifts the saddle and rider away from the horse, creating a greater chance for imbalance.

The overall length of the saddle must also be proper for the length of the horse's back. The rear edge of the saddle jockey must never go far enough back to reach the point of the horse's hip. Short-backed horses should only wear saddles which have had the jockey cut down.

A rider of average size and weight will normally find a 15-inch saddle seat allows enough room for freedom of movement, yet is not too large. When the action speeds up, the rider needs to be able to easily twist her hips to lead the horse into the exercise. The saddle seat should allow the rider to handily make the necessary weight-shift cues and for the horse to recognize such cues. Any restriction caused by a small saddle seat forces the rider into a more rigid, upright position which is ultimately detrimental to both horse and rider.

A smooth swell on the saddle, 12 to 13 inches in width, is most desirable for the western rider who wants to perform a variety of exercises.

All other factors being equal, a lighter saddle from 30 to 35 pounds in weight makes a better working saddle than one which weighs 40 to 50 pounds. Today's show saddles tend to be bulky and heavy, laden with silver. While I'm not opposed to the show-ring glitter, and I certainly understand how eye-catching such silver-appointed saddles can be, I believe that with some thought you can have the best of both worlds. Have a saddle designed so it will not be so cumbersome that it impairs the horse's working ability, yet has enough silver trim to be attractive. A good saddle maker can produce an excellent saddle without using thick, inflexible leather. You can also have a well-designed, well-made saddle which will attract attention simply by being understated.

A second cinch on the saddle, originally designed to keep the rear of the saddle from coming up when a roper dallies, is seldom seen in the show ring. A second cinch serves no purpose for the natural-seat rider, except when roping.

Breast collars are becoming very popular with show riders as another place to put more silver. However, if the saddle fits properly, and if the horse has good conformation and is not overweight, it is not advisable to put a breast collar on a good working horse. There is no way additional straps and weight can be added to the equipment the horse must carry without impairing his natural movement and/or his breathing to some degree. Use a breast collar when necessary to keep the saddle in place on a mutton-withered or low-backed horse.

After taking the horse to the hitching rail or cross ties to be saddled, the rider should first clean the horse's feet, then brush the horse, making sure the hair lies flat and there is no dirt present which might rub against any equipment and cause a sore. The horse should be saddled before being bridled.

Place the saddle pad well up over the withers. Then, holding the saddle by the horn and cantle, and facing the rear of the horse, swing the saddle up over the horse's back and gently lower it into place. The saddle should be a little forward of its best position. By moving both the saddle and the saddle pad back into the proper position, the hair under the pad will be smoothed in the correct direction.

With the saddle in place, lift the saddle pad up off the withers by pushing it gently into the saddle gullet.

Moving to the horse's right side, release the girth and let it drop down. Return to the horse's left side, reach under the horse to bring the girth up into place so it can be cinched with the latigo. The girth should be centered under the horse's body, and it should be far enough back so it does not interfere with the movement of the horse's elbow. Each of the horse's front legs should be pulled forward to smooth the skin under the girth.

Do not try to tighten the girth completely at first. Cinch the horse snugly, then walk him in a small circle several times. Adjust the girth again. I like the girth to be snug, but not tight. You should be able to slip a finger easily between the horse and the latigo.

When bridling the horse, regardless of the style of headstall, the rider should insert the bit gently. The bit should first be warmed or cooled to body temperature and needless to say, should always be clean. Take great care not to strike the horse's teeth.

To insert the bit, grasp the crownpiece of the headstall in the right hand. The left hand is placed under the bit mouthpiece. Standing on the left side of the horse, and facing the same direction as the horse, the rider uses the thumb of her left hand to open the horse's mouth, while the fingers of the left hand lift and guide the bit into the mouth. The left thumb can be inserted in the corner of the horse's mouth. When the thumb is pressed down on the horse's tongue, the horse will open his mouth to accept the bit.

To steady the horse's head in position for bridling, put your right hand and arm over the horse's neck and poll. In this position, the hand and arm help keep the horse's head down, making it easier to insert the bit. With the crownpiece of the headstall near its final position, the bit will hang close to the horse's mouth. Once the bit has been accepted into the mouth, the crownpiece can then be slipped over the horse's ears and into place.

A one-eared western headstall fits over the horse's right ear.

The bit should be positioned in the mouth so it fits snugly in the corners. I don't like to see wrinkles at the corners of the horse's mouth.

The physical construction of the mouth and position of the horse's teeth may require the placement of the bit be adjusted. I like to use the entire length of the bars of the mouth and therefore will regularly adjust the bit placement so the lower, middle and upper portions of the bars are used. To do so sensitizes the entire length of the bar, and prevents a hardening of the bar in a particular spot. The upper portion of the bar is used if the bit fits snugly into the corners of the mouth. If the corners of the mouth are wrinkled, then the bit is often too high, sometimes even lying against the first molars.

Once the bridle is in place, smooth the headstall to be sure there are no twists in the leather and that everything fits snugly, but not tightly. The throatlatch, if there is one, should now be fastened. The throatlatch should be loose enough to permit the head to be brought into a vertical position without the throatlatch becoming restrictive.

The well-trained western horse should be ridden in a curb bit. The style choice is up to the rider. Personally, I like a bit with a moderate, slightly curved shank. I like a bit with some weight to it. The choice of mouthpiece depends somewhat on the amount of the horse's training. The better trained the horse, the more bit he can carry. It takes a well-finished horse to carry a high port or a heavy, bulky port and roller.

Horses are individuals and will like some mouthpieces better than others. It is up to the rider to decide which she thinks is best for the horse.

The bit should hang naturally in the horse's mouth. The design and weight of the bit should encourage the western horse to position his head so a line down his forehead and nose would be vertical to the ground. When the horse's head is carried in the vertical position, the mouthpiece of the bit will be touching but not resting on the bars of the mouth. The weight of the bit will be carried by the headstall.

When the rider moves the reins, the bit should move slightly. A quick response to minimal bit movement indicates the horse has a sensitive "made" mouth, communication has been established and the horse is reacting to the request. The more subtle the request from the rider, the better.

Do not select a bit to control the horse. Select the bit which will most gently deliver your request for action.

Never forget that bits, by design, create discomfort. You want a bit which creates the least amount of discomfort, yet quickly communicates.

Bits do not train horses, control horses or make better riders.

In the final analysis, the bit is not of much importance.

The rider's hands, soft, strong and consistent, create the communication through the reins and bit which elicits the correct response from the horse.

It is how the rider uses her hands which is most important.

The choice of reining styles is up the rider. Neither makes the horse work better or worse. The working ability of the horse is a matter of natural talent.

Regardless of the reining style or the style of bit, the western rider's goal is to tell the horse what gait and what direction are desired. In telling the horse the gait wanted, the rider must understand that the horse's body length changes to accommodate the required length of stride. The horse's body is at its longest when walking, shorter for the jog and shorter still for the lope. At the walk, the horse over strides his front hoof print with his rear foot. The hoof flight is higher and shorter at the jog and there is no over striding. The hoof flight is even move elevated at the slow lope because the horse's body is again shorter due to its more rounded posture.

To begin action, the rider jiggles the reins to tell the horse to direct his attention to the rider--a request for action is about the be given. Then the rider shortens the reins, either in her hands or by a slight lifting, to indicate the gait desired. In telling the horse the gait desired--length of body required--the rider is simultaneously telling the horse the frame within which the horse is to carry himself. The "frame" is an imaginary box surrounding the horse. The rider must decide just how long or short she wants the horse's body to be, then use the length of rein to reduce or extend the frame.

The length of rein determines the position of the bit in acting as a barrier to forward movement. If the reins are long, the horse is being asked to work within an extended frame and there is essentially no bit barrier to forward movement. If the rider shortens the reins, the bit is repositioned and becomes a barrier to forward movement. If the rider is applying leg pressure, asking for forward movement, then the horse must reframe himself to work within the reduced frame size. By shortening his body, the horse places himself on the bit, making the bit position comfortable within the mouth.

The instant the horse responds to the request for a new body position, the rider must release the reins, allowing the horse to remain within the frame on his own. The rider should never hold the finished western horse within the frame by maintaining a constant contact with the horse's mouth.

The rider may frequently bump the horse gently with the bit to remind the horse to maintain the frame position. All such mouth contact must be quick, light and discontinued immediately after a response from the horse.

In riding on a loose rein, without mouth contact, the rider must constantly be aware of the horse's frame. If the horse starts to come out of the frame, it is the rider's responsibility to remind the horse of the desired body position and gait. The rider does this by moving the bit lightly in the horse's mouth while using her legs to request the horse continue the movement.

The rider must be ever alert to the horse's frame. The rider must be sensitive to the feel created by the horse's movement, anticipating any change and taking action to maintain the frame and gait.

The western rider requests specific actions, then after making the request, allows the horse to respond freely. Such request and response is the goal and epitome of western riding.

The training of the western horse is a matter of teaching a communication system which allows the rider to ask for a particular frame, gait and movement. The western horse which has learned the communication system understands the request, takes the required frame and gait and then completes the movement, all free of rider control or domination.

Training is simply the repetition of requests with light confrontation given for incorrect responses and praise for correct responses. Confrontation is never abusive, but is merely the stopping of action, a bump with the bit to reestablish the frame, or an increase or repetition of leg cues to achieve more drive from the horse's hindquarters.

The western rider who requests an action then maintains mouth contact, is penalized in two ways. First, she penalizes herself and her horse because her reactions will never be as quick or as instinctive as the horse's. The horse's performance is slowed and dulled. Second, she will be penalized by any judge who understands the horse should work with freedom and on his own.

Heavy-handed western riders maintain mouth contact for security and as a means of maintaining balance. Such riders become heavier and heavier on the bit and the horse becomes less and less sensitive to any message. The horse cannot concentrate on giving a good performance because he is doing everything possible to escape the discomfort caused by the bit which is applying constant pressure to his mouth.

Every contact with the horse's mouth should be a purposeful communication, followed by an immediate release. There should be no resistance created by the rider, nor resistance on the part of the horse. The horse complies with the request through non-resistance--a relaxing and softening. This is only possible after the rider releases the horse to work with freedom.

The western horse should always be seeking the center of the reins. A slight increase on the side of the horse's neck from one rein or the other should generate an immediate response. The horse should move away from the rein pressure, attempting to find the center point where there is no pressure from either rein.

Responsive neck reining is the result of the rider using her weight and leg aids with each rein request. If the rider wishes to turn to the left, for example, the right rein is gently pushed into the horse's neck while the rider turns her body to the left. The turning of the body shifts the rider's weight slightly into the direction of travel, thus leading the horse. The turning of the body also allows the left leg to drop back and the right leg to move forward. While these legs movements are almost imperceptible, they are all that is needed to lead the horse into the gentle turn to the left.

The western reins must have enough slack so that in making any indirect rein cue, the cueing rein is not pulled so tight that it tips the horse's nose in the opposite direction of the turn. In turning to the left, for example, it is the right rein which gives the indirect rein cue, and it is the right rein which is shortened as it is pushed into the horse's neck and to the left. If the rein is being held too short prior to the cue, the rein will be pulled tight and will create a pressure on the right shank of the bit, thus tipping the horse's nose to the right.

Western neck reining requires the reins remain long and loose. A light, quick, unrestricted response is not possible on a tight rein.

While a long, loose rein is necessary to correctly cue the western horse, it is also a requirement of good western riding that the rider be able to shorten the reins without excessive movement.

The "pitched" or "draped" rein seen in show horse classes are, as so many competition movements, just exaggeration for its own sake. Such exaggerations are not examples of good western riding.

3

Ready for Action

Natural western riding is a partnership in which the rider makes a request, and the horse performs as asked.

It is the rider's responsibility to be sure the horse has been given clear, concise and proper information. If the rider's communication is correct, the experienced horse's response will be correct. If the rider fails to provide the needed information, or fails to give the correct information, only the rider is at fault.

The rider must never surprise the horse with a request, or change requests without first completing the "in-progress" task.

The rider must know what she wants, prepare the horse for the upcoming request, and then know how to properly ask for the desired response.

At rest, the horse is motionless; the reins are loose, there is no mouth contact.

Now the rider wants action. But before asking for a specific and precise movement, the rider must inform the horse that a request for action will be forthcoming. She does this by simply lifting the reins and gently shaking them.

The horse recognizes the movement of the reins as his signal to be alert and ready to proceed.

The rider must now tell the horse what is to be done and at what gait the exercise is to be performed.

The first decision must be the length of rein, for it is the length of rein which determines the horse's frame and gait desired.

If the rider intends to ask for the walk, the rider must immediately drop the reins after having alerted the horse to action so the horse will not shorten his body, but will remain in a long frame. The horse's body will be at its longest when walking, so the rider must keep the reins slack.

With the reins in the proper position, the rider gives the verbal command to walk, then squeezes gently with both legs. The rider should use only her lower legs. With the responsive, advanced horse, it is not usually necessary to use the heels.

If the rider intends to cue with the heels, then she should turn her toe outward so her heel is pressed against the horse's side at the desired position. By turning her toe outward she allows the muscles of her leg to work at their optimum, thus giving her maximum leg strength.

If the rider's toes are facing forward and she attempts to cue with the heel, she will find her lower leg lacks strength and her heel slides along the horse's side toward the flank.

The rider must turn her toe outward in order to cue precisely with the heel. The entire cueing area along the horse's side is no more than 12 inches. If the rider wishes to move only the horse's forehand, the heel cues at the girth. If the horse is to move its body laterally, the heel cue is a few inches behind the girth. And if the rider wants to influence the hindquarters, then the heel is positioned a couple of inches farther back.

All movement of the horse is initiated with the hindquarters, so it is the hindquarters which are of most importance to the rider. The rider must be aware of and able to influence the hindquarters if the rider is to elicit a correct performance.

The leg pressure applied by the rider causes the horse to extend the muscles of the back legs, which moves the horse's body forward. The horse actually loses his balance forward, and reaches out with a front leg to catch himself. Regaining his equilibrium, the processes is repeated and the horse is in forward motion.

The walk is a four-beat gait and the horse moves with his head down, neck extended. **Action can start with the left or right hind leg. If the right hind leg moves first, the right foreleg must move second in order to get out of the way of the advancing right hind which will over stride the hoof print left by the right forefoot. The left hind leg then moves, followed by the left fore. The right hind immediately begins a new sequence and the horse is walking.**

The rider should keep her lower leg lightly against the horse's sides. With the rider's legs against the horse--not exerting pressure, but just resting--the horse remains confident in the work he is performing.

If the legs are removed, it is a signal to the advanced western horse that a new request is about to be made: prepare.

All action, even the walk, initiates in the hindquarters.

Keeping the leg gently resting on the horse's side also allows the rider to apply leg pressure to drive a grounded hind foot, or to apply pressure to further elevate a foot in flight.

It is at the walk the rider should learn to feel the horse's grounded hind foot.

When the horse is walking, the horse's hip will be high corresponding to the foot which is grounded. Conversely, the hip on the opposite side will be low and that foot will be off the ground.

It is important for the rider to always know which hind foot is grounded as the information becomes an intregal part of the communication for many different exercises.

The jog is a very slow two-beat diagonal gait. In the jog, for example, the horse will move both the right hind and left fore together, followed by simultaneous movement of the left hind and right fore.

Diagonal legs move together when the horse jogs.

To make the transition to the jog, the rider lifts her hand just slightly, thereby shortening the reins to ask the horse to shorten his body frame. With the reins shortened, the rider applies very slight and equal leg pressure with both legs and moves her weight very slightly rearward, encouraging the horse to drive his hind legs a bit farther under his body in order to lift the repositioned weight. The horse will round his spine upward slightly, reframing himself. In the shorter frame, the horse must alter his foot flight. The foot flight will not be as long and low as in the walk, but will be higher and shorter in stride length. The instant the rider feels the horse respond to the transition request by reframing himself, the rider must drop her hand, lengthening the rein enough to avoid mouth contact. The horse should work on his own within the new frame. It is the rider's responsibility to keep the horse in frame.

The horse is jogging.

The rider keeps her legs lightly against the horse as a constant reminder this is the gait desired and he should continue in this manner.

Holding the horse in frame or reframing is done in two ways.

The horse will be reminded to stay in frame if the rider simply lifts her hand, thereby shortening the reins for just a fraction of a second. Consistent reminders of this nature are all that the advanced western horse needs to maintain a perfect position while jogging.

A less finished horse may require the rider to use repeated half-halts to maintain the desired pace and body position.

The half-halt is accomplished by lifting the rein enough to establish light mouth contact. While maintaining the mouth contact, the rider must use both legs to squeeze the hindquarters

forward. **The mouth contact is not discontinued
until the rider can feel the horse round its back
upward, thereby slowing its pace. As the rider
releases the mouth contact, she also releases her
leg pressure and the horse is once again allowed
to work within the frame on his own. The young
or anxious horse may require the rider to repeat
the half-halt requests every three or four strides.**

To half-halt the rider lifts her hand and shortens frame.

Repeat the half-halt as often as is necessary.
The exercise is an excellent one for the improvement

of both horse and rider. Half-halts encourage suppleness and recognition of subtle cues.

If the horse jogs slowly, the crisscrossing movement of the horse's body is relatively easy for the rider to sit. However, if the horse moves too quickly (trots), most riders will find it difficult to maintain a deep seat.

The rider must not put weight in the stirrups. The stirrups are held in place by the pressure created in the bottom of the feet when the calf muscles are extended so the heels are lower than the toes.

The moving horse drops out from under the rider, so the rider must sit down on the horse without weight in the stirrups if the rider is to drop when the horse drops. If the rider has weight in her stirrups, the horse will drop below her seat, leaving her unseated. About the time gravity pulls her body down, the horse is coming back up and the bouncing begins.

If necessary, the rider should take her feet out of the stirrups and practice riding until she masters sitting the jog.

The western lope is a three-beat gait in which the action is initiated by the opposite hind leg of the lead desired. For example, if the rider wants a right lead, the first movement of the gait will be a short stride by the horse's left hind foot. The second beat is the right hind foot and the left forefoot moving together. The final beat is the right forefoot in an extended stride.

To request a right lead lope, the rider must shorten the reins as a means of telling the horse a new gait, more elevated than the jog, is required. The rider then shifts her weight toward the horse's

The lope is a three-beat gait requiring rider weight shift.

hindquarters on the left side by simply moving her left hip back. As she is shifting her weight to her left hip, she is also applying pressure with her left leg. Her left leg cue tells the horse she wants a driving action from the horse's grounded left hind foot. The rider's weight over the left hind foot insures the horse's left hind foot will take a shortened stride. The rider's weight to the left side of the horse causes the horse to contract the left side muscles, at the same time extending the right side muscles.

The reining cue for the lope is both the shortening of the rein to reframe the horse and a slight indirect left rein to turn the horse's nose to the right, the direction of travel. There is always a left or right direction of travel and the horse's nose should always be tipping into the direction of travel. Even when riding a straight line, there is an eventual left or right direction of travel.

When the horse begins to lope on the right lead, both the horse's body and the rider's body will be slightly extended on the right side. It is the feeling created by this extension, or leading, which tells the rider instantly which lead the horse has taken. The rider should never lean forward to look for a leading foreleg. Leaning forward changes the communication with the horse, removes the correct cue, and applies unwanted rider weight on a forehand.

The western rider will know by feel within the first stride which lead the horse has taken. The rider should practice lead recognition until it is instantaneous.

As the horse lopes along, the rider must maintain her natural, relaxed body position and the slight lower left leg pressure which reassures the horse he is performing correctly.

The instant the rider feels the horse begin the lope, she must discontinue any mouth contact and allow the horse freedom to work on his own within the requested frame.

The inexperience horse will tend to lift his head and neck more frequently at the lope than at the walk or jog. The rider must be ready to correct the horse as often as is necessary, repositioning the head and reframing the horse's body.

Correction and reframing can be done in two ways. The rider can, with the more experienced horse, simply "bump the bit" with a quick lifting and dropping of the reins. The rider should continue to bump the bit until the horse properly reframes and repositions his head.

If bumping does not succeed in getting the desired results, the rider must use the half-halt. The half-halt is always requested in the same manner, a shortening and holding of the rein position while the rider's legs apply pressure to drive the horse's hindquarters farther under his body. The instant the horse responds by rounding up his back, reframing and slowing his pace, the rider must release the reins, giving the horse his freedom once again to work on his own.

The western horse should work in a relaxed, slow manner at all three gaits.

Working slowly requires great strength from the horse and should not be expected of a green or very young horse. Any horse must be well conditioned--which takes time and continued exercise--to work slowly and within a frame without mouth contact.

If the horse is working slowly and relaxed at all three gaits, it is evidence the horse and rider are truly partners and are in harmony. Adding speed to the work of the western horse is easy, but should never be done until slow work is mastered.

4

Cues to Communicate

As horse and rider advance in their ability to work together as a team, cues will become more subtle, almost imperceptible to any viewer. Mental communication between horse and rider, always followed by a physical response, will soon take over. The outward signs of cues being given will seem to disappear.

This state of quiet agreement is the ultimate goal. It comes only when the horse and rider have mutual respect and trust and are in a state of harmony. Patience, understanding and hours of practice must precede mental communication between the partners. Such a state can never be forced. It is earned and it evolves naturally.

I believe a condition of pure mental telepathy is possible. It occurs when there is a coinciding of both horse and rider's mental patterns which unconsciously generate physical movement.

For example, if the rider wishes to move forward, her thought to do so motivates a physical reaction. She lifts the reins slightly and unconsciously and unnoticeably tightens her leg muscles. The horse simply moves forward because the desire for action is understood. Thus, the rider mentally leads the horse.

When an exercise is learned, the rider will initiate the action by thinking about it and acting in an instinctive physical manner. As the request is communicated through the mental and physical actions of the rider, the horse receives, understands and assumes control over the completion of the exercise.

To achieve this teamwork, the rider leads the horse until the horse receives the message, interprets it and then begins to complete the work on his own.

In any fast action, the horse will be the quicker of the partners. The rider, therefore, must take the leading position in order to remain in balance with the horse as the horse finishes the action. To lead the horse through an action exercise, the rider uses three cues, always given in sequence, yet almost simultaneously.

In sequence, the cues of western riding should always be weight shift, leg movement and finally hands (reins).

Always consider the weight cue first, since weight is always present. Properly positioned, the rider's weight provides the basis for a correct response. If she is improperly positioned, the weight cue at the very least gives an unclear message and at the worst elicits a completely undesirable response.

Let's examine how the cues are used when the rider wishes the horse to move to the right at the walk.

When the western horse is at rest, the reins are quite loose, even dropped down on the horse's neck. The rider signals the horse action is about to begin by gently picking up the reins. With the lifting of the reins, the horse should become alert, but should not move until the rider indicates the type of work, the direction and the gait desired. This is done by using the combination of cues.

With a well-schooled, responsive western horse, the rider need only look to the right (which shifts the rider's weight to the right hip) and at the same time imperceptibly apply pressure with both legs to have the horse move off to the right at the walk.

The finished western horse needs no more instruction than to have the rider think, "I'd like to move to the right at the walk." The rider will then, most often without conscious effort, complete the cues by looking to the right--a movement which in addition to shifting the rider's weight, brings the rider's legs against the horse. The sensitive horse understands the weight and leg pressure and moves in the direction and at the gait expressed by the rider's cues.

The good western rider never attempts to simply rein the well-schooled horse into an action. To do so will cause the horse to lead the rider, leaving the rider behind the motion and out of balance.

The reining of the western horse always follows the weight-shift--which puts the rider into the leading position--and leg cue. Weight and leg cues balance the horse and provide required information never addressed by the reining cue.

There are three basic rein cues for the western horse--the **indirect rein**, the **direct rein of opposition** and the **indirect rein of opposition**.

The principal goal of the western rein cue is to get the horse to seek the center of the reins by moving away from rein pressure. The reins lie along each side of the horse's neck and, when relaxed, do not apply pressure. When no pressure is applied by either rein, the horse is said to be "in the center of the reins."

If the horse seeks the center of the reins, and if the rider correctly relinquishes control to the horse once the action has started, the horse will be in a position to complete the exercise on his own and unencumbered.

The horse seeks the center of the reins as a response to directional cues.

The only other purposes of rein or bit cues in western riding are to inform the horse of an upcoming action, establish or reestablish the correct frame and to act as a barrier to forward movement.

The reins are never held to establish ongoing mouth contact with the western horse. The reins may be pulled and immediately released to "bump the bit" as a means of reminding the horse of the desired frame and head position, or to tip the nose into the desired direction of travel, or even as a disciplinary action. But the reins are never shortened, pulled or held steady, which creates constant bit pressure in the horse's mouth.

As mentioned in Chapter 1, the rider shortens the reins when mounting, taking a basic **direct rein of opposition**. Mouth contact is established and the bit acts as a barrier to inform the horse no forward movement is desired. Once the rider is mounted, the reins are loosened to the point of dropping them down on the neck. The rein position now tells the horse to remain relaxed and resting; no request is forthcoming.

When the rider is ready for movement, the reins are lifted gently, alerting the horse to prepare for action. If the rider wishes to move forward at the walk, the reins are left reasonably loose so there is a slight looping. The bit hangs naturally in the horse's mouth without pressure and the horse is not asked to shorten his frame. With the reins in this position, the horse has been informed the rider has selected the walk as the desired gait. When the rider exerts gentle leg pressure with both legs, the horse will begin walking in a straight line.

The western horse's body will be extended to its fullest length at the walk and the rider does not want to interfere with the horse's natural movement by shortening the reins.

As the horse moves along, the rider may make a decision to turn to the right. In thinking, "I wish to go to the right," the rider looks to the right and this small movement naturally shifts her body weight to the right. With the slight turning of the body, including the shoulders, there is a corresponding natural movement of the legs. The rider's left leg will want to move forward and into the horse as the rider's left hip moves forward. The rider's right leg will want to drop back as the rider's right hip moves back toward the horse's right hip.

The exertion of the leg pressure is minimal, as is the movement of the legs forward and backward. The principle remains true, however, that the left leg, simply through the twisting movement of the upper body, exerts the greater pressure. The western horse, having been taught to move away from the greater pressure, therefore begins a turn to the right. The horse will not fall into the turn, however, as the rider's right leg is held in position and acts as a barrier. The horse will bend around the inside leg.

The western horse will attempt to move away from pressure and to the rider's weight, keeping the weight centered. The horse increases or decreases his speed of movement relative to the amount of weight shift and leg pressure.

The rider delivers the final required information with an **indirect rein**, in this case the left rein pushed gently against the left side of the horse's neck. The horse will move his head and neck to the right, seeking the newly established center point between the reins.

The left indirect rein lies gently against the horse's neck.

If done naturally, indirect reining results in an easy response from the horse. Turns to the right or left will not be made sharply, since no braking action is involved. When the rider uses the indirect rein, it is expected the horse will make a turn no shorter than two lengths of his body.

The **direct rein of opposition** is used as a barrier to forward movement, to slow the horse, to initiate or regain a collected position or to frame or reframe the horse. The direct rein of opposition is achieved by lifting the hand to set the bit barrier, or moving the hand back toward the rider's stomach to establish a barrier.

Direct rein of opposition slows or stops forward action.

As the horse moves forward, the western rider may use the direct rein of opposition to slow the horse. This calls for the half-halt. The rider should shorten the rein by lifting or moving her hand slightly toward her stomach, establishing a very light mouth contact. At the same time, the rider applies light leg pressure with both legs, asking the horse to move the hindquarters farther under his body. The instant the horse responds by rounding his body and slowing his pace, the rider drops her hand back into position to allow the horse to continue on in frame and on his own.

It is imperative the rider immediately release the mouth contact at the first response by the horse.

A green or intermediate level horse may require halt-halt reminders every five or six strides. It is difficult for the horse to remain in frame and work slowly. Slow work on the part of the horse requires much more strength than faster work.

Speed can be added to an exercise at any time. Adding speed is easy. To have a horse work any exercise slowly is the sign of a good rider. It is much more difficult to work slowly than to work quickly.

Collecting the horse is simply a matter of moving the horse's natural balance point toward the hindquarters. When the horse is at rest, the natural balance point is just behind and above the horse's elbow and in front of the rider. To collect the horse properly, this balance point must be moved under the rider. This is accomplished by shortening the horse's neck and chest muscles, driving the hindquarters further under the horse and rounding the spinal column through direct flexion.

The western rider uses the direct rein of opposition to collect the horse. This is done by slowly and gently shortening the reins, but not quite making mouth contact. At the same time the reins are being shortened the rider squeezes the horse with both legs. By using equal, mild leg pressure, the rider is telling the horse to move forward. Since all action initiates in the hindquarters, the hindquarters move first and are placed further under the horse. The horse is said to be "pushed" to the bit. The bit is not pulled back against the horse's mouth, but the horse is pushed into the bit which is held in a fixed position by the direct rein of opposition.

When the hindquarters can move no further forward, direct flexion of the spine takes place--the spine is rounded upward--and, finally, the horse shortens his chest and neck muscles, flexes at the poll, relaxes the jaw and tucks his head into the vertical position.

The horse is now in a collected position with his natural balance point directly under the rider. The moment the horse achieves this position, the rider must lengthen the reins, allowing the horse to remain within the collected frame without mouth contact. The rider will also discontinue leg pressure, but will leave the legs in contact with the horse's sides, assuring the horse he is in the correct position and moving at the correct gait.

The direct rein of opposition is used to tell the horse the rider wishes a shorter body position and therefore a different gait.

When the horse is walking, his body is at its longest, the reins are looped and the horse remains within the frame on his own.

To ask for the jog, the rider need only lift her reining hand slightly to shorten the reins. The horse feels the direct rein of opposition and recognizes he cannot extend past the fixed bit position. The rider applies light leg pressure with both legs, telling the horse to drive harder with the hindquarters. In order to accommodate the rider's request, the horse must shorten his body and change his foot flight pattern. Instead of long and low, the foot flight must take on a shorter and more elevated flight, the two-beat diagonal jog.

As soon as the horse begins his response to the direct rein of opposition cue, the rider must drop the rein, eliminating any mouth contact, and allow the horse to work on his own within the frame.

The lope, which requires the horse to shorten his body and change his foot flight once again, is requested in the same manner, using the direct rein of opposition.

The rider must remember all direct rein of opposition cues are given in combination with leg pressure cues. The horse must be "pushed" to the bit by use of the legs.

The western horse is pushed to the bit and into the desired frame. Now the horse is in the desired position for the upcoming exercise. Once the horse assumes the frame, the rider loosens the reins, expecting the horse not to change his body position, but to maintain it and perform the exercise on his own.

If the horse forgets or loses his concentration, the western rider uses the direct rein of opposition in a bumping action to remind the horse to get back in frame. The contact with the horse's mouth is brief, never a steady pull.

The **indirect rein of opposition** is the most difficult and complicated of the three basic western riding rein actions. It must both brake the forward movement and turn the horse at the same time. The reins must be shortened (opposition) and laid against the horse's neck (indirect), signaling a halt and a turn.

The rein is pushed into horse's neck on left side and shortened at the same time. Rider's hand moves toward right hip.

Correct placement for the indirect rein of opposition in a rollback to the right, for example, requires the rider to move her reining hand toward her right hip. This puts the left rein against the horse's neck on the left side, just in front of the withers, and at the same time also exerts a **direct rein of opposition.**

The rider must be extremely careful that the indirect rein of opposition is not too forceful. Too much pressure will both jerk the horse's head to the left, since the rein is being shortened on the left side, and elevate the forehand, since the horse's forward movement is being blocked by a fixed bit position.

To tilt the horse's head away from the direction of travel is incorrect, as is elevating the forehand. The forehand should remain low, and the horse should move away from the indirect rein pressure.

The opposition pressure must be strong enough to brake the right hind foot, but not so strong as to lift the forehand.

When a rider wants to do a rollback, she starts her communication with the horse by turning her upper body in the desired direction of travel. This turning shifts the rider's weight and begins the positioning of the rider's legs. The rider completes her instructions to the horse by use of the indirect rein of opposition. This conveys the message that braking the hindquarters is required, as is turning to seek a new center point between the reins.

If the rider wishes to roll back to the right, she turns her upper body to the right and looks back in the expected direction of travel. Turning the upper body creates a weight shift which leads the horse into the turn.

The rider's left leg moves forward slightly, signaling to the horse a forehand movement away from leg pressure is required. The right leg moves back toward the flank, indicating that a continuing driving action is necessary. The rider moves her hand toward her own right hip, bringing the left (indirect) rein across the horse's neck to apply indirect pressure while also applying opposition pressure to further forward movement.

The reining movement creates a bit barrier to forward movement, requiring a braking action by the hindquarters. The indirect rein pressure tells the horse to seek a new center point between the reins, which is now somewhere off to the right.

Once the horse has come around far enough to the right to find the center point between the reins, he will discover there is no longer any indirect rein of opposition pressure. The release of all pressure is both the horse's reward for having responded correctly and his cue to relax, yet remain alert for the next series of cues.

How the horse responds to any of the three rein positions depends on his gait at the time. If the horse is walking, a quick response to the rider's weight shift and leg is not required, since both rider cues will be slight. On the other hand, if the horse is loping, he will respond more readily to the cues since they will have greater influence over his natural balance.

In all reining action, the horse's head remains low and the horse stays relaxed only if the rider cues him gently, avoiding any steady pull on the reins. The horse should always comply with the request through nonresistance. The rider cues, then immediately frees the horse from any pressure the instant the horse gives a response. The rider should never be guilty of establishing a continuing resistance.

The use of excessive force, or the maintaining of resistance, will cause the horse much discomfort, and he'll show his displeasure by tossing his head, or worse, resisting the rein pressure and fighting the weight and leg cues.

Although the western rider's goal is to accomplish all exercises with the reins held in one hand, it is a good idea for novice or intermediate riders to practice with a rein in each hand. Holding a rein in each hand assists the horse in learning to seek the center of the reins and helps him avoid the problem of over flexing on one side or the other.

With a rein in each hand, it is easier for the rider to carry her hands low. Low hands encourage the horse to carry his head and neck long and low.

High hands often create a high-headed horse.

The very best western horses have learned to seek the center of the reins and to remain in frame on their own. They are ridden by riders wise enough to never apply unwanted or unconscious rein pressure.

5

Stopping and Backing

The philosophy of natural western riding is probably never more visibly violated than when an unschooled rider becomes a dictator and tries to overpower her horse when stopping or backing. There is no need for force, yet it is frequently employed.

Stopping and backing, as all other exercises performed by horse and rider, are a matter of practice and teamwork, if beauty and balance are to be the result. The rider asks for the stop, cues the horse, then, upon feeling the horse's response, relinquishes control so the horse can finish the exercise on his own. Teamwork, without force, is also the rule for backing.

Good western riding is dependent on cues which are not harsh, severe or surprising. But too often with the novice rider, gentleness is forgotten and the power play begins. The novice rider attempts to jerk the horse to a stop by pulling back on the reins. Similarly, when the novice rider wants to back her horse, she invariably pulls straight back on the reins, applying constant painful pressure.

A direct rein of opposition is used only to reframe, slow or collect the horse. A bit barrier is always released immediately upon a response by the horse.

In stopping and backing, a shift of weight and leg pressure are the principal cues. Reining cues tell the horse what to do with his body and the desired direction of travel. Such reining cues are always subordinate to weight and leg cues.

The western rider must learn the timing and proper feel of a good stop. It takes practice, practice and more practice because a number of cues must be employed and in the correct sequence.

The horse's anatomy is designed for speed and running long distances, not for repeated quick, hard stops. Of course, the horse is capable of making such stops, but even at play he does so infrequently. When he is carrying a rider, hard stops are often made with a great deal of reluctance.

The horse's rear legs are principally driving units rather than well-engineered stopping devices. The rear foot is small and more elongated than round. Its design is for a digging-in type of traction rather than for sliding on top of the ground surface. The fetlocks are strong and flexible, but are not of the best design to lock and hold the weight of both horse and rider for relatively long periods of time. The fetlocks work best in spring-like fashion. The hocks are susceptible to injury from strain and are under severe stress during a hard, sliding stop.

The horse which has a short hind cannon bone and a low set stifle joint will usually have an advantage in making hard, sliding stops. Measure from the point of the elbow to the ground and from the midpoint of the stifle joint to the ground. If the stifle joint to ground is the shorter distance, then the horse usually tends to be a natural stopper.

Generally, the western horse with equal distance measurements from elbow to ground and midpoint stifle joint to ground makes the best all-around athlete.

Regardless of the horse's conformation, we expect the western horse to stop quickly, and sometimes to slide a long distance. (The long sliding stop should be reserved for the competition reining horse, bred for such action and shod with "sliders" which help keep the foot on the surface of the ground. Reining horses should both practice and show on ground specially prepared for sliding stops.)

In stopping, the expectation is that the western horse will plant both hind feet, stop quickly and slide at least a short distance. To accomplish such action, it is incumbent upon the rider to give cues correctly so the stopping exercise remains as safe and easy for the horse as possible. There is always the danger of possible injury with any hard, fast exercise. However, if the rider avoids any attempt to overpower the horse and force compliance, the danger will be lessened, since the horse can work to his own natural ability.

Since slide stops cause tremendous stress on the horse, reining and stock horses have a tendency to "burn out" quickly. It is the wise rider who saves the slides for the show ring, and practices form and position from the walk, jog and slow lope. Once the horse knows how to stop, he will slide-stop. There is no reason to break the horse down by continually asking for unnecessary stresses. A rider with faith in her knowledge and ability will also have faith in her partner's willingness to respond to her requests.

Any well-school horse with ground manners will know what the verbal command, "Ho!" means. The foal should have been taught the command by the time he was a month old. All during his early training, the horse should have been taught to stop, stand and not move once the command, "Ho", has been given. If the horse did not respond immediately to the verbal cue, he should have been schooled with a physical cue--jerk and release on the lead or longe line.

It is completely logical, both for horse and rider, that the first cue in stopping a horse when riding is the verbal command, "Ho!" The command accomplishes two things at the same time. First, it informs the horse more cues are coming, be prepared, and second, it tells the horse what he is expected to do. It is a reinforcement of his early schooling, and it eliminates the possibility the horse will be painfully surprised by a request he was not prepared for.

The rider must employ the introductory cue--the verbal command--then wait until she feels the horse react. It takes a fraction of a second for the horse to receive the message, digest it, send the correct instructions to the muscles, and then have the muscles react correctly to produce the requested action. When the horse understands the "Ho" cue, he'll begin to react, and the horse's reaction will be reinforced positively by the rider's further cues.

The second cue by the rider will be a tightening of her stomach muscles, dropping the

pelvis back and down and locking her seat in the saddle. This muscle tightening should also cause the rider's upper body to incline slightly forward. This is the most desirable position for a rider during a slide stop. The rider should never throw herself back in the saddle to stop. Such action puts her out of position and invariably results in a jerk on the reins. Leaning back to force a hard stop may seem a natural tendency, but it is the action of a rider thinking of overpowering her horse and forcing compliance instead of simply asking.

If the rider maintains tight stomach muscles, she will not fall forward or lean backward. To do either is impossible if the stomach muscles remain contracted.

At the same time the rider is tightening her stomach muscles and locking her seat in the saddle, she should be removing any leg pressure from the horse's sides. She stops riding.

It is helpful to both the horse and the rider if the rider will push her feet slightly forward and brace herself for the stop.

Finally, the rider takes the slack from the reins, establishing a bit barrier to hold the horse within the frame desired.

The rider does not pull back hard on the reins; to do so applies painful bit pressure to the horse's mouth.

The slack, and nothing more, is taken from the reins. The horse stays behind the bit barrier because he has been told to stop and because the rider has stopped riding the horse forward.

At the walk, the horse moves in a four-beat lateral gait, never having both hind feet off the ground at the same time. Giving the verbal request

The horse's forward momentum creates the "slide."

to stop, and then tightening the stomach muscles and removing all leg pressure will result in the horse stopping with one hind foot in front of the other. The horse's reaction and lack of forward momentum allows the grounded foot, at the time the stop was initiated, to remain grounded. The hind foot, which was in flight when the request was made, continues and often extends even farther than normal as the horse prepares to plant that foot for the solid stop.

When jogging, the horse has a different, more elevated foot flight and increased impulsion--power from the hindquarters. These factors allow the very responsive and energetic western horse to jump under himself at the stop, and he will often skid squarely with both hind feet.

At the lope, the horse has a great deal more forward moving inertia, and both hind feet are off the ground for a fraction of a second. When the horse stops from the lope, he'll react to the verbal command and physical cues, but will in addition have to react to his own forward thrust. In order to stay behind the bit barrier, which established his frame, the horse will have to bend his spine upward in direct flexion.

The rider must avoid pulling back on the reins, but should hold the fixed hand and bit barrier, allowing the horse to round his back and balance himself on his hind feet.

By not interfering with the horse, the rider also allows the horse to continue to walk with his front feet, keeping himself in balance and moving forward with the slide of the hind feet.

As the slack comes out of the reins, and the horse moves to the bit barrier, there will be some mouth contact. This is acceptable when the horse is moving to the bit.

However, it is even more desirable to have the horse remain in frame during the stop, avoiding any mouth contact.

If the horse stops on the verbal command and the physical cues of the rider, and the horse remains in frame, then no slack need be taken from the reins.

The advanced western horse can and will stop on a looped rein if a foundation of understanding has been established and practiced repeatedly.

Training Tip
Whenever loping, just before stopping, the rider should apply mild leg pressure with both legs. The leg pressure creates greater impulsion from the hindquarters, but even more important, increases awareness of the rider's cue which is removing all leg pressure.

The good western rider never pulls back on the reins as a request for her horse to move backward.

Pulling a horse backward is always wrong and results in the horse opening his mouth, tossing his head upward or tucking his head to his chest, all efforts to avoid pain.

Backing is accomplished by changing the horse's natural balance, then applying leg pressure to create movement.

The horse naturally stands with about 60 per cent of his weight on his forehand. This is the perfect position for an animal who survives by rapid forward movement over distance. The forehand is a catching mechanism for mass being driven forward by the power of the hindquarters. The forehand is designed to carry weight. At the same time, the hindquarters are designed to push weight forward.

When not in movement, the horse wants his hindquarters unburdened and ready to propel him out of danger at any moment.

To change the horse's natural balance, the rider must shorten the reins gently and slowly. This is very different from pulling back on the reins. The rider, sitting upright and centered, shortens the reins with her hands, never using her arms for power.

At a certain point, the horse will, on his own, shift his weight to his hindquarters. The movement is subtle, but easily felt by the rider.

Once the horse shifts his weight to the hindquarters, the rider must leave her hands exactly where they are and the reins at exactly that length.

If the rider has made no changes, and the horse remains with his weight on his hindquarters, then every request for movement will result in backward movement.

To move backward--a two-beat diagonal gait just as the jog--the rider simply needs to squeeze gently with both legs. The horse will respond to the leg pressure and move backward. If the rider removes her leg pressure, the horse will stop. If the rider reapplies leg pressure, the horse will again move backward. The horse will continue backward until leg pressure is removed, or the reins are lengthened.

If the rider removes her leg pressure the horse will stop. If the rider then lengthens the reins and applies leg pressure, the horse will move forward.

If, while the horse is moving backward, the rider lengthens the reins and continues her leg pressure, the horse will change direction and begin moving forward.

Training tip

Once the horse has shifted his weight to his hindquarters, it is helpful to the horse to have the rider stand slightly in her stirrups. By standing in her stirrups, she removes her weight from the horse's back, making it easier for the horse to round his back upward.

Having horse shift weight to hindquarters is backing key.

In b... ...of travel can be
changed v... ...ein pressure or a
combinatio...

It is... ...e rider to guide the
horse's dir... ...ing her legs. Direct
the hindq... ...and follows. If the
rider wan... ...o move to the right,
left leg pr... ...tly behind the rider's
body pos... ...ns are simply held
against th... ...right side. The reins
block an... ...d movement. If the
rider wan... ...o move to the left, she
applies l... ...blocks any forehand
movemer... ...direct left rein.

If... ...desired, then the rider
would p... ...s in the direction of
travel ar... ...ove the forehand with
the rein... ...e rider wants to turn
sharply... ...moving backward, the
rider w... ...arters to the right with
left leg... ...ng the forehand to the
left witl... ...essure.

...nd left or right while
moving... ...simply needs to apply
indirec... ...it a response. The horse
will m... ...cue while continuing to
respor... ...essures which are calling
for a t...

To negotiate obstacles while backing, it is often necessary for the rider to use a complex set of compensating cues to match the circumstances. In some cases it may even be necessary for the rider to stop all the horse's movement.

Backing around and through obstacles will be examined in the section on mastering trail courses.

Backing the western horse strengthens the horse's hindquarters, giving him greater power, and making it easier for him to perform.

It is always best to keep the horse working well within himself, never asking for so much that the horse is under excessive strain. Backing properly requires the horse to round up his back, get his hindquarters farther under his body and use his loin and stomach muscles. Stretching and strengthening these muscles makes all other work easier.

Backing immediately after nearly every stop will quickly get the horse thinking "back." When he thinks he'll be asked to back after stopping, he tends to plant his hind feet farther under his body by making sure his weight is back on his hind legs.

Because he is thinking "back", he stops better, and because he stops better he is ready to back immediately. One exercise helps develop perfection in the other, so not only is it good practice, it is good training.

The western rider will also note that the horse which backs quickly and with relative ease, has a much easier time loping slowly. His increased ability to move forward slowly is a direct result of his strengthened hindquarters.

Well-executed stops are never forced; neither is correct backing.

The rider should never pull back on the reins and maintain a constant mouth contact in stopping or backing. The serious western student insures both exercises always enhance the partnership.

6

Weight Shift Cues

Unlike your legs or use of the reins, your weight is always an aid in action and can never be eliminated. Therefore the rider's weight must always be considered, and as a cue, must always be correct.

Not only is weight always a cue; it is always the first cue given to a western horse.

Instructors of the classic style of equitation advise the rider to not twist the upper body or lean into a turn. Their goal is to have the rider keep the upper body erect at all times, and the rider's weight in the center of the horse's back.

I suspect they do not have complete faith in the horse's ability to distinguish and respond freely and correctly to a number of subtle cues.

On the other hand, western trainers and riders believe the horse is extremely capable, and smart enough to easily interpret several cues at the same time. In fact, western riders expect the western horse to understand and respond correctly when the rider's weight is shifted away from the direction of travel, and then to interpret and respond correctly when the rider's weight is shifted into the direction of travel.

When the western horse is doing any type of lateral (sideways) work, such as a sidepass, the rider shifts her weight away from the direction of travel. When forward movement is involved in a turn, the rider shifts her weight into the direction of travel.

The classically-trained horse is expected to work with precision and very little speed, while under the rider's control. The western horse is expected to work just as precisely, free of rider control, and with speed, grace and balance.

The western rider must indicate what she expects of the horse by providing an understandable cue. Then she must assist the horse by leading him into the exercise and at the same time free the horse to work on his own.

By twisting the upper body and/or leaning into the desired direction of travel in making turns, the rider both leads the horse and positions herself to be in balance with the horse when the horse moves at his own speed to complete the request.

In western riding, no rider can remain seated in the center of the horse's back, give the cues for a spin and then expect to stay in balance with the responsive, well-trained reining horse. The horse will simply be too fast for the rider. The rider will be left behind and become a hindrance to the horse.

The rider therefore must learn to turn her body and lean into the direction of travel. The turning of the body shifts the rider's weight, placing it naturally in the correct position to assist the horse. The rider must master the cues for slow, basic turns and suppling exercises before she can go on to more advanced riding patterns.

The rider's weight must be to inside on hind pivot foot.

The western horse will move away from pressure and toward a shift in the rider's weight if the horse is moving forward. By moving toward the weight shift, the horse is bringing himself and his rider back into balance. The horse moves under the weight shift in an effort to support the weight.

As we have already established, all action originates in the horse's hindquarters, and all rider requests for action are initiated by leg-pressure cues. The cue should be a pressing one, rather than a kicking motion. The horse should feel the pressure of this cue first from the calf of the rider's leg. If this pressure is not sufficient to evoke the expected response, the rider may then apply greater pressure by using more of the lower leg. The maximum pressure results from use of the heel.

To give strong leg-pressure cues, the rider should turn her toes out and press her lower leg and heel into the horse. By turning the toes out, the lower leg is brought fully against the horse's side and the rider has greater leg strength. Turning the toes out to cue the horse also aids the rider in maintaining a deep seat, with her legs extended down as far as possible, and her heels remaining lower than her toes.

Do not try to keep the toes parallel to the horse when cueing. When the toes are pointing forward, the rider has virtually no leg strength. Worse than just being ineffective, if she attempts to keep the toes forward, the rider often gives a miscue when her legs slide back toward the horse's flanks.

Turn your toes outward for the most accurate leg-pressure cues.

Of course, it is correct to keep the toes almost parallel to the horse's side when the rider's legs are at rest.

If the horse is moving satisfactorily at the walk, then the rider has only the lightest leg contact with the horse's sides. This contact is not the result of any squeezing action by the legs, but is the natural contact experienced when the riders is well seated and relaxed. The legs are at rest, and therefore the rider's toes are naturally positioned parallel to the horse's body.

The cues then for a simple turn to the left are a slight turning of the rider's body as she looks in the direction of intended travel. As the rider turns to the left, her weight will be shifted slightly to the left, and her left leg will tend to want to drop backward. As the left hip moves backward, the rider's right hip moves forward, naturally placing the rider's right leg against the horse at the girth. As the right leg moves against the horse, the rider's right foot will naturally turn outward, and the heel will turn

Turning the body places rider's legs in cueing position.

inward. These actions are in conjunction with a right indirect rein pressure which asks the horse to move left as he seeks the center of the reins.

If the rider simply thinks, "I want to turn to the left," then looks where she wants to go, all of the cues--weight shift, leg pressure and rein--happen naturally and without effort.

Without consciously thinking about correct cues, and without trying to stop any of the body movement which has been initiated naturally, the rider will discover all the cues are correct and easily interpreted by the horse.

The simple desire to turn to the left results in the rider automatically giving all the cues necessary to inform the horse that a left turn is desired. If the responses to the thought occur naturally, rather than being forced, all the cues will be perfectly placed. The rider will find there is never a need to force cues or strain to reach proper cue positions.

Force or unnecessary effort is usually the result of the novice rider's attempts to hold back natural movement or over-cue the horse to compensate for a lack of confidence in the horse's ability to respond correctly.

Natural western riding does not require the rider to force the horse into position. If the horse has been well-schooled and understands the request, he will, by his own nature, assume the correct position.

After the horse has turned to the left or right to the degree desired by the rider, the cues are discontinued as the rider looks straight ahead--the direction of travel. With the natural cues discontinued, the horse is content in the knowledge there is no leg pressure to move away from, no weight shift to move toward and he is in the center of the reins.

The rider can make circles by giving the exact same cues used for a left or right turn, except that the cues are held until the horse has completed a single circle or several circles. In making circles with any braking action, the rider should remember not to turn the horse in a distance less than two body lengths of the horse.

If the rider turns the horse in less than two body lengths, then the rider must then use an indirect rein of opposition rather than an indirect rein. The indirect rein of opposition is used to slow or stop forward movement and turn at the same time.

The offset is a turning exercise in which the rider uses the indirect rein of opposition to keep the horse from more than slight forward movement while turning the forehand 90 or 180 degrees left or right. If the offset is to the right, for example, the rider looks to the right, shifts her weight into her right hip, allows her right leg to drop back and her left leg to move forward while she uses the indirect rein of opposition to rein the horse to the right. The horse will respond to the cues first by moving his right hind foot forward a few inches and then establishing it as the pivot foot as the rider's weight is shifted to it, forcing it to the ground. The horse uses his other three legs to push his body around the pivot foot. The left indirect rein of opposition tells the horse to seek the center of the reins, which is now moving to the right, and at the same time, tells the horse not to move any farther forward.

In the offset, the horse should elevate the forehand slightly and swing his body smoothly to the right as long as the rider's cues are not too forceful. The offset loses its smoothness when the rider's cues are too rough and severe.

If the rider wants a quarter turn (90 degrees), she barely turns her upper body. If a half-turn (180 degrees) is desired, the rider must turn her upper body to a greater degree.

Offsets will require an indirect rein of opposition.

As the horse responds to the weight, leg and rein cues, the rider will determine the degree of the offset by making sure her weight will be centered on the horse at the moment the horse reaches the desired distance. If the rider wants a half-circle offset of 180 degrees, then she must continue her own weight-shift, leg and rein cues until just before reaching the finish point. Just before reaching the 180 degree point, the rider stops her weight shift and centers her weight, while releasing the other cues. The horse will stop the offset exercise the moment he feels he has moved under the rider's weight, reestablishing a balanced partnership.

Training tip: To teach the offset it is helpful to "rock" the horse back and forth, left, then right, before asking for a quarter or half turn. Make the rocking cues (simply left and right turning cues) gentle and rhythmic. If the cues are not light, the horse will respond by bouncing erratically.

Normally the offset is considered a fast exercise in which the horse lifts the forehand and swings it in one motion of approximately 90 degrees. As with all western riding exercises, however, the rider's responsibility is to make the cues as gentle and subtle as possible while making sure they are completely understood by the horse. The rider must never attempt to force speed.

Speed, grace and balance develop as the horse and rider learn to work as a single unit. The rider initiates and the horse completes.

The greatest mistake a western rider can make is to believe she can force the horse into a better position than the one the horse will assume naturally.

If it is ever necessary for the rider to control the ultimate positioning of the western-trained horse, then one of two failures has occurred. The horse has not been properly informed and educated as to what is required, or the horse simply does not have the natural physical ability to perform at the level desired.

In most cases, the training is at fault. In a few cases, the horse simply cannot attain the level of performance sought.

Western-trained horses which become champions do so because they have superior ability. No amount of training can create that ability. Training only affords the opportunity to express the horse's natural talents.

It is the rider's responsibility to help the horse reach his potential, whatever that may be, and never push the horse beyond his physical capabilities.

7

Bending and Suppling

Control of the intiating action for any exercise is the responsibility of the rider, who asks the horse for a particular response by giving the proper cues. Recognizing the horse's understanding of the request, the rider relinquishes control, allowing the horse to complete the exercise.

It is this freedom which makes possible the quick, smooth, natural action of the western horse. If the rider attempts to control the entire action, the horse is hampered. If the rider fails to present her request adequately, then the horse cannot be blamed for failing to complete the action confidently.

The technique of requesting action and then relinquishing control applies to such exercises as the shoulder-in, renvers, travers and rollback, as well as the pivot on the forehand or hindquarters. Mastery of these exercises indicates the rider is progressing well and learning to share the responsibilities of performance with her partner.

The shoulder-in, the travers and the renvers are deomonstrations of the rider's ability to position the forehand and the hindquarters independently of each other, yet at the same time. These exercises are accomplished most easily, if the rider holds the reins in two hands when first teaching the horse. However, when the horse fully understands the exercise, the rider should ride with the reins in one hand.

The terms "in" and "out" always refer to the center of any circle. If the horse is moving to the left to any degree, then the center of the circle is to the left. The **travers (haunches in)** therefore requires the haunches to be moved to the left. The **renvers (haunches out)** requires the haunches to be move to the right. In an arena, the center of the arena is always "in" and the rail is always "out."

A shoulder-in exercise requires the horse to move the forehand the width of the horse's chest to the inside of the circle. The horse's head and neck should bend just a little toward the center of the circle. The hindquarters, however, must rack in a straight line.

If the shoulder-in is being done properly, a person standing in front or behind the horse will see a definite three-track pattern. For example, in moving to the left, the horse's left forefoot, the foot closest to the center of the circle, will make the first track. The horse's left hind and right fore will track on the same line, the second track. The horse's right hind will tack alone, farthest from the center of the circle, the third track.

To position the horse for the shoulder-in, the rider must maintain her weight in the middle of the horse, her spine being directly in line with that of the horse. The rider's left leg will drop back toward the horse's flank to hold the hindquarters straight. The rider's right leg must move slightly forward and press the horse at the girth to push the forehand over the width of the chest. The rider must rein the

Shoulder-in shows three distinct foot-fall tracks.

horse a little to the left, asking the horse to bend his
neck in toward the center of the circle.

When initially practicing the shoulder-in, the

rider will find there is a tendency to exert too much leg or rein pressure in an attempt to force the horse to move into position. Generally, the horse will respond to this by starting to circle instead of continuing in a straight line. Sometimes the horse will let his hindquarters swing out, away from the rider's inside leg pressure. The rider may find it necessary to make any number of compensating cue adjustments to keep the horse in the three-track position.

If the horse begins to circle, the rider will have to soften the rein cue and move the inside leg cue forward to retard the circling action. If the hindquarters should swing away from the inside leg pressure instead of being held by it, the rider will have to correct the horse's position by moving the outside leg cue back toward the horse's flank.

During the learning period, the rider may be required to continue the compensating cues for some time until the horse both understands the exercise and is physically able to perform it. It must be remembered that the shoulder-in, renvers and travers require the horse to arc his spine. This flexion of the spinal column, while not significant in degrees, is difficult to hold for a horse that is not well-conditioned.

However, when the horse is physically able to do the exercise and understands what is being asked, it is the same lateral spinal flexion which tells the rider the performance is correct. The rider will be able to feel the horse's spine arc as the flexion slightly twists the rider's lower body.

If the rider is on an unresponsive horse, she may find it necessary to bump the horse with her heels to bring the horse into position. This must be done carefully or the horse will change gait immediately, become frightened or simply circle. For this reason, it is incumbant upon the rider to keep the cues as gentle as possible.

The rider should always begin every request with the lightest possible cue, increasing the pressure of the cue until there is a response. Each time an exercise is requested, the rider begins with a minimal cue, following it with a little more severe one, and than a more agressive cue until the horse makes an attempt to perform correctly. As both members of the team gain greater understanding of their respective responsibilities, the cues will become more subtle.

The travers (haunches in) is accomplished by the rider maintaining her weight in the middle of the horse, cueing with the outside leg back toward the flank, bringing the inside leg forward toward the girth to hold the forehand straight, and applhing light direct rein of opposition to fix the bit so the horse does not bend his neck.

When viewing the travers from the rear, the observer should see the horse's hindquarters move the width of the hindquarters toward the inside of the circle. In moving to the left, the horse's left hind foot will track alone closest to the center of the circle. The right hind foot and the left fore foot tract together, and the right fore foot tracks alone, farthest from the center of the circle.

The rider will experience the same exaggerated reaction from the novice horse, and again, she must adjust the cues to compensate for the horse's inexperience. If the forehand gets out of

Haunches in shows right fore and left hind on same track.

position, the rider must change one or the other of her leg cues to bring the forehand back to the center. If the hindquarters fail to move over the prescribed distance, the rider may have to bump the hindquarters over by application of greater heel pressure.

The renvers (haunces out) is simply the reverse of the travers, and the rider's leg cues will be just the opposite of the travers cues when the horse is moving in the same direction.

Once she has learned to give the proper cues, then feel the horse's correct response, the rider will be able to exert independent control over the horse's forehand and hindquarters at will.

The rollback, another suppling exercise, is one which requires continuous movement by the horse, making it necessary for the rider to provide an introductory cue, followed by immediate freedom.

When rolling back, the horse begins the exercise as he would begin a stop. Then the horse steps forward with the inside hind foot and rolls his body back over that foot so he is facing in the opposite direction. A horse can do a rollback from the walk, jog or lope, but must always continue the same gait after his direction has been reversed.

To accomplish a rollback, the rider must begin by pushing the horse to the bit, which is then held in a fixed position. The rider squeezes with both legs, tightens her stomach muscles, and shifts her weight a little back and toward the intended turn. The rider does not pull back on the reins, but leaves her hand fixed as she would in stopping the horse.

As the horse begins to stop, the rider exerts stronger inside leg pressure, driving the inside hind leg forward. At the same time, the rider must change her outside leg cue to move

the forehand around and over the horse's inside pivot foot. To move the outside leg forward, the rider must turn her body to the inside and shift her weight to the inside and slightly backward. The reining cue is a light indirect rein of opposition, both turning the horse and stopping the horse's forward movement at the same time.

As the horse recognizes the cues, he'll come around, reversing his direction and repositioning his body under the rider's weight. Both horse and rider will be in balance when the horse has completed the 180-degree turn.

As soon the rider recognizes the horse has

Rollback is a continuous movement of stop and turn.

understood the cues and is positioned to complete the rollback satisfactorily, she must release all cues, providing the horse with the freedom he needs to finish the exercise.

When the horse has completely reversed his direction, the rider will apply the correct set of cues to reestablish the same gait which preceded the rollback. If the horse was jogging, for example, the rider should immediately apply equal leg pressure to reestablish the jog.

A rollback may be made to the left or right from a straight line movement, no matter the gait.

If the horse is moving at the lope, then the rider must make two cue adjustments after the conclusion of the exercise to put the horse on the correct lead. If the horse is moving to the left and rolls back to the right, the rider's left leg is at first forward, pushing the horse's forehand to the right. The rider discontinues all cues as the horse finishes the exercise and starts to come out of the rollback. Since the horse rolled back to the right, the horse should begin his new work loping on the right lead. This requires the rider to immediately inform the horse of what is required. The rider shifts her weight from the right to the left, and applies left leg pressure telling the horse to take the right lead.

Between the completion of one exercise and the beginning of another, the rider should pause, discontinuing all cues. This brief respite is all the horse needs to understand that one exercise has been finished and a new one may be forthcoming.

Training tip: ***With forward-moving, forehand-hindquarter control exercises, practice***

at the jog. The jog is the easiest gait for the horse. Once the exercises are mastered at the jog, then they can be worked at any gait.

Rider cues for the pivot on the hindquarters are often determined by the horse's conformation and natural ability. Some horse's have strong hindquarter muscles and a skeletal configuration allowing them to establish and hold a rear pivot foot easily. Others have a difficult time establishing the pivot foot and holding it throughtout a 360-degree turn.

If the horse has a strong hindquarters and the rider wishes to pivot to the left, then the rider begins the exercise with a weight shift to the left and to the rear. By shifting the weight to this position, the rider has forced the horse's left rear foot to bear more weight than the other feet, inhibiting its movement.

If the left hind foot is not already forward of the right hind foot, then the rider must apply left leg pressure back toward the flank to get the horse to step farther under himself, establishing the left hind foot as the pivot foot.

Right leg pressure toward the girth (to move the forehand to the left) is then applied by the rider, as is light, indirect rein pressure. There should never be any opposition rein pressure. Pivots and spins on the hindquarters are actually forward movements and it is incorrect for the horse to step or rock backwards. The horse should respond to the indirect rein and move slowly to the left, seeking the new center of the reins and avoiding the light right leg pressure.

The rider will have to adjust her cues if she finds the horse is weak in the hindquarters and wants to swing his hindquarters to the right to avoid both the rider's left leg pressure and the necessary slight spinal arc.

Instead of applying continuous left leg pressure to drive the horse's left hind foot forward, the rider will apply left leg pressure, then immediately release it. Such a cue gets the horse to move the foot forward, while discontinuing it keeps the horse from moving the hindquarters off to the right. Instead of applying right leg pressure at the girth to moved the forehand to the left, the rider applies right leg pressure back toward the flank to keep the hindquarters in position.

With this set of leg cues, the rider must rely to a greater extent on the indriect rein cue to move the forehand to the left.

Eventually, when the horse has truly learned to neck rein, pivots and spins will require very little or no leg pressure, and will be accomplished with simple indirect rein pressure.

The rider should keep her weight over the pivot foot. However, if the horse is having great difficulty holding the pivot foot, the rider may want to reschool the horse by shifting her weight to the side opposite the pivot foot, then use leg pressure to push the hindquarters over onto the desired pivot foot.

The pivot requires no speed on the part of the horse and therefore needs only gentle cueing from the rider.

When asking the horse to pivot on the forehand instead of the hindquarters, the rider must first fix the bit as a barrier to forward movement. The rider must not pull back on the reins, but must shorten them to establish light mouth contact, then squeeze the horse forward to the bit.

When the horse is on the bit properly, the rider will ask for a pivot on the forehand with leg-pressure cues only. If the rider wishes the horse to move his hindquarters to the right around his forehand, she uses left leg pressure back toward the horse's flank. The rider must hold with the right leg by positioning the right leg forward near the girth. No right leg pressure is required. The right leg simply blocks the horse from moving his forehand to the right. The leg cues are just reversed for a pivot on the forehand to the left.

The horse should be standing relaxed and quiet before the rider requests either forehand or hindquarter pivots.

8

Cues for More Advanced Riding

Once the rider has learned the cues for forehand-hindquarter control exercises, and she can recognize the feel of the correct response by the horse, she is ready to advance to the halfpass, the sidepass, spins and flying changes of lead.

The halfpass requires the horse to move forward and sideways at the same time. While performing the halfpass, the horse must keep his body straight. As the horse moves down the line, if halfpassing to the right for example, the horse's left legs will cross over and in front of the right legs. The horse will be moving on a diagonal, maintaining a straight body.

In halfpassing, sidepassing and flying changes of lead, just as in **two-tracking,** the rider will shift her weight away from the direction of travel, rather than into the direction of travel. This change in weight cue is always done with lateral work (exercises in which the horse is moving sideways) which does not require speed. When the horse is working with speed, as in a spin or rollback, for example, the rider will shift her weight into the direction of travel. The rider also leads the horse with a weight shift when no lateral movement is required.

In two-tracking, an exercise which requires the horse to position his body at a 45 degree angle to the direction of travel, the rider shifts her weight to the side opposite the direction of travel.

If two-tracking to the right, the rider will hold the forehand in place with a blocking indirect right rein, while pushing the horse's hindquarters to the right with left leg pressure.

Two-tracking sets horse up for halfpass, flying changes.

When moving to the right while two-tracking, the horse crosses his left legs over and in front of his right legs.

The cues for the halfpass require the rider to move her weight to the side opposite the direction of travel. If she wants to halfpass to the right, she will shift her weight slightly to the left, apply left leg pressure just behind the girth and then hold the horse's body straight by not applying a reining cue. The horse is in the center of the reins and the rider wants the horse to remain there.

If the horse does not move to the right in response to the rider's weight shift and leg cue, then the rider may be required to apply indirect left rein. If indirect left rein pressure is necessary, the rider will most likely be required to move her right leg forward to block the horse's shoulder and keep the horse from starting a turn to the right.

Halfpassing can be done at the walk, jog and lope, and will be very easy once the horse learns to move away from the rider's weight shift. Halfpassing is not a difficult exercise for the horse, but one which requires constant practice if the horse is to remain responsive to the weight shift away from the direction of travel. If the rider is careful not to apply a reining cue, then the horse will soon understand the rider is not leading the horse into a turn, but instead is seeking lateral movement.

The correct halfpass movement is an excellent exercise to establish a good foundation for the flying change of lead. The flying change of lead, when perfected, is requested by a simple shifting of the rider's weight. The cues, timing and positioning for the flying change of lead will be discussed later.

The sidepass also requires the rider to shift her weight away from the direction of travel.

The classic style of riding teaches the rider to always shift weight into the direction of travel. Such action when lateral work is involved inhibits both horse and rider.

If the rider wants the horse to move to the right in a lateral action, the rider should have her weight on the left side of the horse, pushing with the left leg to move the horse into unrestricted space.

In the classic style, the rider would shift to the right side of the horse, becoming, in effect, an obstacle in the horse's path of movement. While shifting her weight into the direction of travel, the rider must also attempt to push the horse to the right with a weakened and ineffective left leg.

Such action is unnatural for both horse and rider, and I suspect while advocated, is never practiced by master riders.

To sidepass, the horse should be standing still and relaxed. The rider should lift the reins to inform the horse a request for action is forthcoming. When the horse responds, the rider will shorten the reins to set the bit as a barrier to forward movement. The rider then shifts her weight to the left, if the sidepass is to be to the right, applies light left leg pressure and light left indirect rein pressure simultaneously.

While the horse is learning, the rider will be required to make an exaggerated weight shift, and may also need to apply quite strong leg pressure. As the horse's work becomes more refined, the weight shift should become so subtle it will not be noticed by a spectator.

As the horse begins to move away from the left leg pressure, the rider may find the horse attempting to turn his head and neck to the right.

Rider shifts weight to side opposite direction of travel.

(A horse should always have his nose tipped slightly into the direction of travel.)

The rider must hold the head and neck straight, and she does this with indirect right rein pressure. The rider must be on constant alert, always ready to make compensating corrections to keep the horse moving within the proper frame.

In sidepassing, which is uniquely a western movement, the horse must cross both the fore and hind legs. If they cross correctly, the left fore and hind legs will move in front of the right legs when the horse is moving to the right. The opposite is the case if the horse is moving to the left. It is difficult for the horse to make a perfectly straight lateral movement since the horse cannot laterally bend his legs below the elbow or stifle joints. The horse must therefore swing his leg out from the shoulder and the hip. If the horse is restricted by the rider, he'll be unable to swing the legs out far enough to cross without striking or stepping on the opposite leg.

In sidepassing, the horse should be balanced equally on his forehand and hindquarters. It is best if the horse makes a perfectly straight lateral movement. If the horse encounters great difficulty with the sidepass, it is acceptable for the forehand to slightly lead the hindquarters.

Training tip: In the early stages of training, practice moving the forehand, then the hindquarters. As the horse becomes more receptive to the cues, begin trying to move the forehand and hindquarters together. If the horse makes mistakes, go back to the basics and reinforce the foundation work.

When sidepassing, the western horse will continue a smooth, steady movement until the rider stops the action. The exercise can be ended by the rider simply returning her weight to the center of the horse, relaxing the leg pressure and dropping the reins. The horse should come to rest immediately.

The rider should first use reining cues to correct any misplacement of the horse's body rather than using leg pressure cues. For the horse, leg pressure cues are more closely associated with pivots on the forehand or hindquarters, and the horse may easily misinterpret extra leg cues as blocking instructions.

Training tip: Making a box figure by walking the horse forward, then sidepassing to the right, then backing and finally sidepassing to the left is an excellent way to make the horse responsive to weight shift and light leg cues. An advanced horse should be able to make the box three or four times without stopping his motion.

Spins are difficult for many horses, so it is important the rider select spinning cues which will give the most assistance to the particular horse being worked.

When a horse spins, the sequence of leg movement should be such that there is an equal loading on all four feet so the horse is prepared to stop the spin at any point and move off immediately in a straight line.

In spinning to the right, the sequence of leg movement should be a short forward step with the right hind foot (the pivot foot). Then a pushing movement to the right is required by the horse's left front foot, which will cross over the horse's right front foot. Another sideward/backward movement by the right front foot will catch the horse and reestablish balance, and finally a sideward whipping

The spin is a forward movement starting with a turn.

action by the left hind foot will conclude the sequence. In the spin, only the horse's front legs cross.

The spin is actually a forward movement, so the rider must be careful in setting a bit barrier that she does not pull the horse backward. Many trainers begin the horse's leg sequence with a sideward/backward foreleg step in the direction of travel. This is acceptable as long as the horse is not

Rider's weight should be toward pivot foot during a spin.

being pulled backward and the pivot foot has been properly positioned under the horse.

To spin the horse to the right, the rider must have the horse take a short right hind step, establishing the pivot foot. In stopping that foot's forward flight, the rider stops the horse's forward movement and redirects it into the flat lateral action of the spin. If spinning to the right, for example, the rider positions the right hind foot as the pivot foot by applying left leg pressure to get the horse to drive off the left hind foot, thereby moving the right hind foot off the ground and forward. As the right hind foot is coming forward, the rider shifts her weight onto the horse's right hip, grounding the right hind foot. With the weight shift, the rider turns her upper body into the direction of travel which brings her left leg forward so she can push the horse to the right. The rider's right leg will drop backward, but should not apply pressure.

Most importantly, the rider applies indirect left rein pressure. The horse should immediately begin to seek the center of the reins, moving the forehand to the right. When first teaching the spin, it is helpful to use the reins in two hands. The right rein should not pull the horse into the spin, but should only tip the horse's nose to the right. As frustrating as it may be at the beginning, the horse must be taught to move away from the indirect rein pressure and quickly seek the center of the reins. Response to the rein rather than the leg is what makes the spin flat and smooth.

The spin is created by the rider simply keeping the center of the reins just to the right of the horse. The horse will keep seeking the center of the reins until the rider stops the action by blocking further movement with a stationary indirect right rein.

The spin should be a flat movement in which the horse's body is nearly straight. The horse's nose should be tipped in the direction of travel, but the horse should not bend his neck--rubberneck--in an effort to avoid moving the forehand. The rider must not pull back on the reins, causing the horse to overload his hindquarters and possibly back out of the spin.

With some horses the rider may find it necessary to use a slightly different set of cues to spin correctly. A horse which is conformationally weak in the hindquarters will have a tendency to swing the hindquarters away from the forehand's direction of travel. We call this "swapping ends."

If this is the case, then the rider must hold the hindquarters in place, or even more radically, push the hindquarters onto the pivot foot. If the rider wants to hold the hindquarters, then, when spinning to the right, the rider must use left leg pressure back toward the flank to keep the hindquarters from moving to the left. This action is acceptable if the horse is actively moving away from the indirect left rein.

There are horses which require the rider to push the hindquarters over onto the pivot foot. When this is necessary, the rider will use a very strong left leg pressure toward the flank to push the horse onto the pivot foot, then move the forehand with the indirect rein.

When pushing the hindquarters over the pivot foot, the rider may find her right leg tends to move forward as her body is working hard on the left side. The rider must be careful not to allow her weight to shift to the left side, grounding the left foot instead of the right.

As with all other western riding exercises, once the rider has initiated the exercise and is sure the horse understands what is expected of him, the rider must relinquish control to the horse. If the horse is truly responsive to the neck rein, and is given freedom to complete the exercise, he'll do so in good form.

It is when the rider attempts to force speed or fails to yield control that the horse will back out of the spin, swap ends, jump around or throw his head up.

Training tip: A good way to teach the basics of a spin is to jog the horse in a very tight circle. Do not let the horse bend around your inside leg. Make the horse keep his body straight, tipping only his nose into the direction of travel. Be sure the horse is turning because he is moving away from the indirect rein cue.
Reduce the circle until the horse is turning around his pivot foot, crossing his front legs and maintaining a straight body. When the horse has completed several turns over the pivot foot, immediately walk him forward.

A flying change of lead is a natual movement for the horse, so it requires more in the way of timing than in active cues. The two cues needed are a shift of weight and a switch of the rider's leg aid.

A brief summary of the movement of the horse's legs at the lope will show us why the timing of cues is so important.

The lope on the right lead is a three-beat gait in which the action is initiated by the horse's left hind foot. The second beat of the gait is the right hind foot and the left fore foot moving together, and the third beat is the leading right fore foot.

Just as the leading right fore foot is being grounded, the horse has both hind feet off the ground for a brief moment. This is the moment in which the horse can change perfectly within the three-beat sequence. To assure the horse has the opportunity to make the change, the rider must begin her cues while the leading fore foot is in the air. This allows the horse ample time to understand and respond to the cues.

If done correctly, the rider's weight shift causes the hind foot on that side to ground early, thus creating a new loping lead. The change of the rider's leg cue simply reinforces and confirms that the horse is moving correctly.

To put the horse on the right lead, the rider shifts her weight back and to the left to establish a shortened left hind stride. The rider allows her right leg to move slightly forward toward the horse's right shoulder. This is a natural movement by the rider and precedes the natural extension of the horse's muscles on the right side.

The rider should allow very gentle indirect left rein pressure to inform the horse the direction of travel will be to the right.

When the horse is on the right lead, all of the horse's muscles on the right side are extended. This twists the rider's body slightly and pushes the rider's right hip forward. In this position the rider is able to feel the horse is on the requested lead. The rider should never look down at the horse's shoulder or lean forward to look for the leading fore leg. Doing either puts both horse and rider out of a balanced and natural position for the exercise.

Timing is the most critical element in requesting a flying change of lead. If the rider asks too soon or too late, the horse is not in a position to make the change in a single sequence of leg movements. If the rider's timing is off, the horse will often change in front, but fail to make

the change behind until the following lope sequence.

On right lead, the second beat, right hind and left fore, is completing, as right fore begins its forward movement.

By asking the horse to change while the leading forleg is in flight, the horse has the opportunity to make the change behind first, then complete the lope sequence with a change of leads in front.

So as the leading foreleg is coming forward, the rider gently lifts the reins to slow and gather the horse, while shifting her weight from one side to the

Leading right fore is planted as hind feet pass in mid air. Rider makes change by switching weight to ground the right rear.

other. If the horse is on the right lead, the weight shift will be from the left hip to the right hip. As the weight transfer is being made, the rider must let her legs follow naturally, the right leg going back and the left leg moving forward. A light indirect right rein tells the horse he is now on a gentle circle to the left.

All of the cues are given simultaneously.

The rider's weight shift causes the horse's right hind foot to be grounded first. The rider's right leg pressure informs the horse that his right hind leg

The change has been made to the left lead and the horse prepares to finish the three-beat sequence by extending left fore.

is to pick up the driving action instead of the leading action, and the indirect right rein pressure tells the horse the new direction of travel. Done correctly, the change of lead will take place in one smooth movement of a single three-beat sequence.

Too often rider's try to force the flying change by throwing the horse off balance and into a new direction of travel, or by using extreme leg cues. Such actions result in the horse resenting his work.

All that is required is that the rider inform the horse with gentle cues at the correct time, then give

On the new left lead, the horse is quiet and in frame.

the horse the freedom necessary to respond. No forced, harshly demanded flying change will be as smooth and graceful as the horse's natural change.

Training tip: First be sure your horse always takes the requested lead on a straight line.
Then practice counter-canters--loping to the left on the right lead, loping to the right on the left lead. While counter-cantering ask for a flying change of lead, and the horse will most often be very happy to oblige.

9

Mastering Trail Courses

No matter what event you choose for your western horse today, you cannot ignore breeding and conformation when selecting a prospect.

The most successful trail class horses will most likely come from identifiable families, and all will most assuredly have similar conformation and disposition characteristics.

Your trail horse prospect cannot be willful in temperament. He must be the kind of horse that is willing to accept his rider's guidance and direction through obstacles. The horse which says, "No way, I'm outta here," simply won't make a good trail horse.

Look for a big, soft eye in your prospect.

Horses have relatively poor eyesight at best and must contend with having both monocular and binocular vision. So selecting a horse which has a better chance of seeing things clearly means you are selecting a horse which is less skittish, and that goes along with having a better temperament.

A horse with a big, soft eye is generally a kind horse, which means he is generally more trainable.

You want a trail class prospect which has "a natural step." A natural step refers to the horse stepping easily through the trot over and lope over distances. Watch your prospect trot and lope over ground poles and evaluate his step.

A horse with a short step will have to reach, so he must be taught to extend his step. A long-striding horse will have to be taught to shorten his stride.

Teaching a horse to extend is much easier than teaching a long-striding horse to shorten, because a horse is much less comfortable maintaining a short frame.

A natural step is best, of course, but either a short step or long step can be corrected with training. And in either case, the horse will not have to maintain a particular frame for long periods of time. Once the horse has worked a particular obstacle, there is usually a change of gait.

The cadence of your horse's stride will be taught; however, natural ability makes everyone's job easier.

A horse with a high level of curiosity will stay interested and have a good expression when showing. This is not something you can train into a horse, so look for this characteristic before purchasing. The curiosity trait is an added bonus, and you want all the advantages you can get.

Good trail class horses are careful with their feet. A horse which does not want to hit ground obstacles will make the training process much easier. Horses that just don't care about bumping things will eventually cost you in competition. Teaching cadence can help, but it will not always save you.

A quiet horse is a good choice. The quiet horse will not become rattled in difficult or new situations. You don't want a nervous horse which worries and frets. The nervous horse makes too many mistakes.

You can get the quiet horse to increase his level of attentiveness, but the nervous horse is very difficult to keep under subtle control.

Finally, choose a small to medium sized horse. Trail horses must work within confined spaces and a short-coupled, small to medium horse will be much more comfortable collecting and maintain a short frame. Large horses can certainly collect well and do the work. But once an obstacle has been set, that is the size you must work in and you get no allowance, no matter how big the horse.

The first step to winning competitive western events is to pick a horse which has the natural talent it takes to win. Each competition class is different, requiring a different kind of horse to be a champion of that event.

You want the best possible partner. And your partner wants a partner smart enough not to ask the impossible.

Know The Basics

Before beginning work on trail class obstacles, your horse will have to know the basics. These include walking, jogging and loping in a collected manner, backing, side passing, pivots on the hindquarters, turns on the forehand and being able to turn so his hindquarters track his forehand.

When I say the horse needs to be able to walk, jog and lope in a relaxed manner, I mean he must perform all three gaits while maintaining balance and collection. He cannot be tense, or stiff in the back so that he falls into his turns or fails to show suppleness and an ability to leg yield (bend and move his body in response to leg pressure).

To do these things well, your horse must be in good condition and strong enough so that any performance requested is well within his ability. The horse should never have to work hard at his exercises. If he is well-conditioned, he may breathe a little quickly after performing certain work, but his recovery time will be short, and his energy level will remain high.

The horse ready to begin trail class work will be smooth in both upward and downward transitions. If the horse has to lift his head to go from the walk to the jog, or the jog to the lope, then he isn't well enough conditioned, and/or he doesn't yet understand he is to remain in frame.

Being able to back straight and stay straight while making turns is an absolute must. The horse should be fluid when backing, not dragging his feet or moving in a herky-jerky way. He should be able to back slowly and stop immediately when asked.

Side passing in both directions should be easy for the horse. If the horse is balky or stiff, he is not ready to begin trail class work. More polish is needed.

The horse should be able to pivot on the hindquarters both left and right. The horse which has mastered pivots will move off the rein cue and will cross his front legs. If moving to the left, the right front leg should cross in front of the left front leg, and vice versa.

Turns on the forehand, left and right, demonstrate the horse is responsive to the rider's leg cues, and that the rider has good control over the horse's body.

Turning will be perfected with training. In the beginning, the horse should follow his nose around and should have some understanding of neck reining.

The horse should respond to the rider's weight shift, moving in the direction in which the rider is looking. When the rider turns and looks in the intended direction of travel, for example, to the left, her weight shifts slightly into her left hip, her left leg drops back slightly and her right leg moves into the horse at the girth. The horse should respond by turning under the rider's weight and away from her right leg pressure.

A horse which turns his nose away from the direction of travel, or one that allows his body to fall into a turn, is not ready for more advanced work.

The western horse is ready for trail obstacles when he can remain collected and balanced during turns.

Neck Reining

Neck reining is the epitome of western riding, a skill which, when mastered, completes your horse's trail class training. How well the horse responds to the reins will often be the single factor between an average performance and a superior performance.

Even though neck reining may be considered the finishing touch on a well-schooled horse, I want to emphasize that neck reining skills are introduced almost with the first ride. They are honed with each training session, and so you must have a complete understanding of neck reining even before you begin teaching the horse his first trail class basics.

When the horse neck reins properly, he stays between the reins. We say he seeks the center of the reins. The cue from the rider is very slight. The horse will place his head in the correct position with a very slight bend in the direction of travel. If the horse is moving to the left, for example, the horse should have his nose to the left, just enough to allow the rider to be able to see the horse's left eye.

The trick to teaching neck reining is to ride the horse just as if he were a perfect neck reining horse. Ride the horse as much as possible just as if he were already a finished horse competing for a championship title.

Plow reining or direct reining--pulling on the left rein to pull the horse's head toward the left--teaches the horse to respond to a direct pull. This is not what you want. It does just the opposite of teaching the horse to neck rein. Plow reining, or pulling the horse's head into the direction of travel, also causes the horse's head to rise out of position and allows his shoulder to fall into the direction of travel.

Teaching the horse to neck rein should be an every day exercise. The rider should think about it constantly.

When the horse is carrying a snaffle, the direct rein is used to tip the horse's nose into the correct position and direction of travel.

The indirect rein should be placed against the horse's neck. Think of the indirect rein as "pushing" into the horse's neck. Your indirect rein hand should not cross over the center line of the horse's neck.

For example, if you are moving to the left, the left rein is the direct rein and it tips the horse's nose to the left. The right rein is the indirect rein and it is pushed into the horse's neck on the right side.

The rider turns and looks in the direction of travel which means her weight shifts to the left and her left leg is held against the horse, holding the horse and keeping the shoulder upright rather than falling into the turn. The rider's right leg will be used to push the horse into the turn if the horse is not turning. The right leg reinforces the initial indirect rein cue.

Do not use more rein cue. Use more leg pressure if the horse is not responding.

Practice turning just with the rein; apply leg pressure only when needed.

While introducing the horse to the curb bit, ride with two hands. Keep your hands close together so it seems to the horse that only one hand is holding the reins. Teach the horse to respond to the neck reining cue just as you did while the horse carried the snaffle.

Large easy turns should be calm and show your horse has a good understanding of his required body position.

Use obstacles to help the horse. You can serpentine around ground poles, making the turns tighter and tighter. The good trail class horse will be able to make very tight turns and remain upright and balanced. When making tight turns, be sure to use enough inside leg to hold the horse's shoulder up.

Always keep in mind the indirect rein must not come across the horse's neck. The indirect rein is pushed into the horse's neck.

Keep the horse on a relatively looped rein, allowing the horse to use his neck for balance, as well as dropping his head to look at obstacles lower than his knee.

When you think you are ready, and the horse is responsive to indirect rein pressure, begin riding with the reins in one hand.

Be prepared to help the horse with the direct rein if needed. But only help the horse by correcting his nose position; don't pull him through the turn.

Often a horse's head will get out of position because the rider is crossing over the horse's neck with the indirect rein. When this happens the indirect rein tightens to the point it becomes a direct rein, pulling the horse's head in the opposite direction of the turn. Do not cross over the horse's neck with the rein. Always push the rein into the horse's neck.

The rider's hand should move only a few inches right or left when turning. Do not pull your hand back toward your hip, creating a indirect rein of opposition. The indirect rein is used for turning. An indirect rein of opposition is used when stopping forward action and turning at the same time.

The more the horse understands how to seek the center of the reins, the more you should ride him as a finished horse, a western neck reining horse.

The more he is ridden as a finished horse, the more polished he will be.

Obstacles--things you'll need

For training, you will need at least four of each length of ground pole. Plan on having 12-foot poles, 8-foot poles, 6-foot poles and 4-foot poles.

Poles should be painted in stripes of various colors. Following the colored stripes makes it easy to find your path through the obstacle. Special obstacles can be grouped by using poles striped with the same color.

You'll need a dozen pylons or cones, the size of which does not make a great deal of difference.

It will be necessary to construct a bridge. For training, the bridge should be six feet long and four feet wide. (It is sometimes handy to have a wider bridge for young, inexperienced horses. Once your horse learns to walk a wide bridge, he won't hesitate to walk a narrow one.)

You will need a water box. Make it large enough for the horse to be able to do a complete 360 degree turn. It is not necessary for the depth to be any greater than four inches. Don't forget to make the box seams water tight.

A gate which opens both ways is a necessity. You may also want to create a gate which is nothing more than a strand of rope between two poles.

Blocks or risers are used to elevate poles and other obstacles. You may need as many as a dozen, since most of the time you use blocks or risers in pairs.

Be sure you have plenty of plants. Live plants are nice, but they are heavy to transport and are often short lived. Silk plants give your horse the experience of working within shrubbery, but he won't be so inclined to take a nibble, and you won't have difficulty moving them about to create different arrangements.

Measurements

The following measurements are the approved distances for American Quarter Horse Association shows. If you show under other breed association or organization rules, be sure to check the rule book.

The spacing for walkovers will be 20 inches to 24 inches and may be raised to 12 inches.

Elevated walkovers should be set at least 22 inches apart.

Trotovers shall be 3 feet to 3 feet 6 inches apart and may be elevated to 8 inches.

Lopeovers shall be 6 feet to 7 feet and may be elevated to 8 inches.

Obstacles which must be backed through are to be spaced a minimum of 28 inches in width. If the back through is elevated, then the width must be increased to 30 inches. The elevation of a back through may be no more than 24 inches.

If the course requires you to serpentine at the jog, then the obstacles must be at least 6 feet apart.

The minimum width for a bridge is set at 36

inches. The length of a bridge should be at least 6 feet.

The poles over which a horse must sidepass may be elevated to 12 inches.

While the measurements listed here are for AQHA competition, I have found most horses are very comfortable with a 2-foot space for walkovers, a 3-foot space for trotovers and a 6-foot space for lopeovers.

Getting Started
Walkovers, Trotovers and Lopeovers

The more relaxed a young horse is, the more he will learn.

Horses are relaxed when they are familiar with their surroundings and have confidence in both themselves and their rider.

So I think the best way to start with a young horse is to be sure he never knows he is getting started.

Place a few single poles around your arena. Most of the poles should be scattered with no pattern in mind. Have several other poles at measured distances. I like to start with poles six feet apart because these can be trotted or loped over.

Begin by walking your horse toward a pole. Aim for the center of the pole, and keep the horse moving in a straight line. As you approach the pole, roll forward slightly on your thigh to inform the horse walkovers are coming. Getting weight off the horse's back allows the horse to lift his feet higher.

If your horse wants to stop and look at the pole, that's fine, but you want to encourage forward motion.

Once the horse is crossing the pole comfortably at the walk, you are ready to jog. When jogging over poles, the rider sits quietly in a balanced position.

Master a series of poles at the jog, before advanced work.

Ride the arena and establish a balanced jog with good rhythm. When the horse is moving comfortably, ride over a single pole. Keep riding at the jog. When the horse will cross a single pole without signs of concern, cross a single pole, then immediately find another pole to cross.

When the horse is confident jogging the unpatterned poles, you can begin walking over the series of measured poles.

If the measured poles are six feet apart, then your horse will be able to take two jog steps in between poles.

Gain your horse's confident, and be sure he is completely relaxed jogging over a series of measured poles before you even begin to think of lopeovers.

During your horse's lessons of jogging over poles, you can give him a mental break by changing gait and loping over a single pole now and then. By the time you are ready to lope over the measured poles, your horse will not suspect it is a new lesson.

Whether walking, jogging or loping, be sure to establish a good cadence and have your horse collected and balanced.

Do not look down at the poles. Looking down shifts your body weight and interferes with your horse's ability to maintain a steady cadence and stride.

Increase the difficulty of your lessons by adding more poles.

The poles must be a measured distance apart, but can be in many forms, such as a four-sided box or semicircular fan.

When it is time to again increase the difficulty of the work, tighten the path the horse is to take. Having tight turns before approaching a pole makes both horse and rider think, plan and concentrate. As the horse masters the walkover, trotover and lopeovers, raise the poles with risers or blocks to in-

Fan formation adds difficulty to lope or jog overs.

crease the difficulty.

Training tips:

When teaching walkovers, do not use protective leg gear. When the horse feels the sting of hitting a pole, he'll learn on his own to pick his feet up.

After the last walkover, count each foot step, one through four, and then stop. Stand for 30 seconds or more. This teaches the horse patience, and he will soon learn not to hurry through walkovers since he knows he is just going to stand and rest at the end of the exercise.

Have a long set of 8 to 10 poles to help teach the elevated step. It is important to keep moving forward. Don't let your horse stop while in an obstacle.

Establish a forward jog. Often a western pleasure jog is too slow and short. In order to feel the rhythm and establish a good cadence, count the front footsteps as they hit the ground. The count will be 1-2-1-2-1-2.

Look up, never down at the pole.

Leave your horse alone while he is going over a pole. Your horse should be concentrating on the pole, not being interrupted by a message--intentional or not--from you.

It is your responsibility to establish the cadence and keep the horse on the correct path. You are partners with your horse, and it is your horse's responsibility to get you over the obstacle; don't get in his way.

Look up. The most common mistake made by riders when working lopeovers is to look down.

Count the front footsteps beginning with the leading foreleg as it hits the ground. The count will be 1-2-1-2-1-2, and it will help you to establish cadence and feel the rhythm.

The horse must keep his shoulders up, so the rider needs to establish light inside leg pressure, around which the horse can bend. When riding trail classes, the rider does not lean into turns.

Cadence

Cadence means measured movement, such as dancing or marching.

Having cadence at the walk, jog and lope is extremely important in trail classes. You cannot win at the highest levels if your horse does not exhibit cadence.

If a horse is moving with cadence, each step is the same. This must be done while riding on a loose rein, as is done with all good western riding. To be able to maintain cadence, the horse must be in good condition, that is to say have the strength to remain collected and in frame for a period of time.

When a horse performs with cadence, a trail class which has measured obstacles will be much easier. Always practice obstacles which have been correctly measure, for this in itself helps teach cadence. The horse should not chip (short stride) or reach (long stride), but should maintain strides of the same length.

To teach cadence, create a large circle of poles correctly measured in six-foot spaces. Use about 30 poles. Place four or five poles six feet apart, then have no poles for the next 18 feet, then set three more poles at six feet apart. Then create a 12-foot space before setting two or three more poles. Allow another space of 24 feet without poles, and then set four or five more poles six feet apart. Continue until the circle is complete. Measure carefully from the center of one pole to the center of the next pole. Be sure the measurements are correct. The center is your path.

Begin riding at the jog. The jog is a three-foot step, so between the poles, the horse's front legs will take two steps before stepping over the pole. Count to yourself, 1-2-1-2-1-2. In the 12-foot space, the horse will take four steps with the front legs before stepping over the pole.

By knowing the distance and how many steps the horse should take, you can test yourself on the cadence. In the 12-foot space, if the horse takes five steps, then his step is too short. It is your responsibility to lengthen his stride. If the horse is only taking three steps, then his stride is too long and must be shortened.

At the lope, with the poles set six-feet apart, the horse's front feet will take only one step before going over the pole. In the 18 foot distance, the front feet will strike the ground three times before stepping over the pole.

Ride the horse around and around the circle to establish cadence and learn the correct steps.

For the more advanced horse, raise the poles to increase the difficulty.

The rider has two tasks. The first is establishing the cadence, and the second is taking the correct path. The rider must know the distances and how many steps are to be taken. When the rider establishes the correct cadence, the obstacles are easier for the horse.

It is very important for the rider to establish the cadence prior to reaching the obstacle. When approaching the obstacle, the rider must know the exact path--the points from which the distances are measured. By knowing the path the rider knows the required steps, then can establish the cadence.

If the rider does her job, then the horse can do his job and the partnership is perfect.

Walkovers, of course, also require cadence. The walking step is two feet. Practice poles set with two-foot spaces are the easiest.

To increase difficulty, set a six-foot box. The horse should step three time within the box before stepping out. Working a 12-foot box is even harder. The horse should step six times with the front feet before stepping out.

Teach the horse to walk slowly with a short step. A horse in a hurry will usually lengthen his step.

Keep three things in mind and mastering trail obstacles becomes much easier:

1. Establish cadence.

2. Know the path and direct the horse.

3. Leave the horse alone and let him work the obstacle.

Turn Around in the Box

There are a couple of little tips you must know to work a turn around in the box.

First, understand that the turn around is just that, a very small circle within the box. It is not a pivot.

The horse should be arched in the direction of travel and both the forehand and the hindquarters need to move equally. The reins guide the forehand and the legs guide the hindquarters.

When entering the box, step in and start turning. This keeps the horse's forward motion going and it looks smoother to the judge. After completing the turn, stop and let your horse establish his balance before stepping out of the box.

The rider should look at the center of the box when entering, and then look to the inside of the turn. The rider's body should stay in the center of the box. If the rider finds herself close to the edge, then an immediate adjustment needs to be made.

Turn around in a box means turning in a circle.

To increase the difficulty of the obstacle, jog into the box and stop. The horse must stop on voice

142

command and a release of leg pressure to do this more advanced maneuver.

Training tip: When jogging into the box, be sure to look at the center of the box. That is where you want to stop. If you look at the far edge of the box, or outside the box, that is where you will go!

The box should be made of six-foot poles and is always square.

To make the exercise a little more difficult raise the poles.

And if you really want to test your skills and your horse, put plants at various spots around the box.

Backing, Side Passing

When working a back through obstacle in competition, i.e., you back your horse through the established obstacle, your horse should move slowly, but with no hesitation. Each step counts. Extra steps or lifting and replanting the foot will be penalized.

To perform a back through successfully, your horse needs to be able to back straight, turn on the forehand and pivot on the hindquarters. You must be able to move the forehand or hindquarters independent of the other.

Begin your back-through training with two parallel poles set four feet apart.

Practice backing straight between the poles. Keep your legs close to your horse to give him support and control his body movement.

Slow, steady movement is required in back-throughs.

If a correction is needed, make the correction while the horse is taking a step backward. This makes the correction more subtle and prevents the over correction.

Always keep your horse's head straight and be sure the horse is paying attention to you. If the horse is looking around while the rider is looking back, the horse is very apt to turn his body. Be aware of the horse's head and head position.

Center horse's hind feet in turn when backing an "L".

When backing through an "L", back the horse so his hind feet are centered in the turn. This will position the cantle of your saddle at the end of the long inside pole. Stop when correctly positioned, then use the turn on the forehand to move the horse's hindquarters over 90 degrees. Stop for a moment, then use the turn on the hindquarters to move the horse's forehand 90 degrees, positioning you for the final straight back movement. Stop and wait a second or two before backing straight out of the obstacle.

Training tip: In practice, do not always back completely out of the back-through. Back to the end, then walk forward and out. This helps keep the horse from rushing his back through.

To back around barrels or cones, use the same techniques. Back straight, then stop, and use the turn on the forehand or the turn on the hindquarters to position the horse properly for the next backing action.

Always keep your legs close to your horse when backing. The light leg contact gives your horse a feeling of security and helps prevent overly large steps to the left or right.

Go slow. When backing, you want to be sure your horse is always in a good position, never up against an obstacle. Take a step or two, then stop. Repeat the exercise.

When you are in a competitive situation, the backing movement should be in slow fluid steps. And your horse must stop when told to stop. Never allow the horse to take an extra step backward.

Be sure you always know where your horse's feet are. To see exactly how much clearance you have, you will have to look down at the horse's feet. But when you look down, you always look down from one side, and you always look down by looking behind your leg. If you look down on one side only, there is little chance your weight shift will cause the horse to step incorrectly, as moving from side to side often does. And if you look down behind your leg, your upper body stays almost straight rather than leaning forward.

If your horse's foot is too close to a pole, correct it during a backing step. As the horse steps back, push the hip over gently. This prevents over correction.

Start the horse's training with easy, wide backing obstacles. As the horse learns, you can make the obstacles more difficult by making the back throughs tighter, or by raising the poles.

Side passing, when done correctly, is a side step with a forward weight shift by the horse. When moving to the right, for example, the left fore and the left hind legs must move in front of the right fore and right hind legs.

The most important element of side passing is getting the horse to be comfortable while crossing his legs.

Practice side passing without a fence line or other barrier. Working a box shape is a good exercise because the horse must walk forward a few steps, then side pass to the right, for example, then back as far as he walked forward, then side pass to the left. All of this in one exercise makes the horse very responsive to weight shifts and the application and removal of leg cues.

When you are side passing in competition, be sure you are looking in the direction of travel

and that you look behind your leg when viewing obstacles on the ground.

In a show class, the rider wants to remain in the center of the horse as much as possible. A slight weight shift to the side opposite the direction of travel is acceptable as it will help the horse. But it is best to have the horse working more off your leg cues than from the weight shift. By staying straight and balanced in the saddle, the cues are more subtle, the movement smoother and the picture the judge sees is perfect.

Side passing requires horse to cross in front and behind.

When working an obstacle, the side pass should be smooth and continuous. Do not let the horse side step, then stop, then side step and stop again.

When side passing over a pole, the pole should be centered under the horse. To be sure the pole is centered, the pole should always be just behind the rider's leg.

When first starting a horse side passing over poles, begin by stepping over the pole, then side passing off.

As the horse improves, approach the pole by side passing to it. Then side pass over it and off. To provide more difficulty, side pass around turns, such as around a box.

If working a box made of poles, work first with the horse's front feet inside the box, then with the hind feet inside the box. Side pass to the corner of the box, then use a turn on the forehand or a turn on the hindquarters to negotiate the corner.

Pivots, Turns on the Forehand

Pivots (turns on the hindquarters) and turns on the forehand are essential maneuvers that will be used in back-through obstacles and when working gates. Pivots and turns on the forehand allow you to make movements more precise and accurate.

To perform a pivot on the hindquarters, the horse must have his weight very slightly back and on the pivot foot. When turning to the right, for example, the right hind foot becomes the pivot foot, and the sequence of strides would be right hind foot planted as the pivot foot, left forefoot crossing over in front of the right foreleg, then the right forefoot moving into position to catch the horse's mass as it is propelled to the right by the left hind foot pushing. The right hind foot essentially stays in one spot, and the horse moves around the pivot foot. To keep from twisting the joints of the right hind leg, the horse will lift the pivot foot and reposition it during the regular sequence of strides.

The horse's head should remain straight in front of the horse's body with only a very slight tip of the nose in the direction of travel. The horse's shoulders should remain elevated.

To cue for the pivot to the right, stay sitting in the center of the saddle and simply turn slightly and look in the direction of travel. You want the horse to move slowly and evenly, so use a light indirect left rein to neck rein the horse around the turn. The left leg may be used to push the horse around, but it really shouldn't be necessary.

To perform the turn on the forehand, the horse must be standing with equal weight on each front foot. The forehand will remains relatively stationary while the hindquarters move. If moving to the left, the right hind leg should cross in front of the left and vice versa.

Begin cueing for the turn on the forehand by applying leg pressure to move the hindquarters. At the same time use an indirect rein to block forehand movement. If moving to the right, for example, the left leg pushes the hindquarters around while the right rein is used to block the forehand from moving to the right. The blocking indirect rein must not be pushed into the neck, rather it should be gently placed against the neck.

Gates

There are eight ways to work gates.
1. Right hand push and walk through.
2. Right hand pull and walk through.
3. Left hand push and walk through.
4. Left hand pull and walk through
5. Right hand push and back through.
6. Right hand pull and back through.
7. Left hand push and back through.
8. Left hand pull and back through.

When walking through a gate, always stand facing the latch. When backing through, always stand facing the hinges.

It is the horse's job to position the rider so the gate may be worked easily. The side pass, pivot, turn on the forehand, backing and neck reining are all used in working a gate.

To work the right hand push and walk through, begin by standing parallel to the gate facing the latch. Pick up the latch with your right hand. Back a few steps slowly so the horse's head is past the gate standard. Using the neck rein, guide the horse through. Once your knee has passed the end of the gate, begin pushing the horse's hindquarters toward the left until the horse is facing the opposite direction. Now close the gate by side passing to the right.

Gates require variations of turns, pivots and side passes.

A right hand pull requires you pull the gate toward your horse as the horse side passes to the left. When the gate is well open, move your horse forward until you knee is just past the end of the gate, then neck rein the horse to the right and walk him through. Push the hindquarters slightly to the left to close the gate, then take a few steps backward so you can latch the gate.

On a left push back through, you will start facing the hinges of the gate. Push the gate open and push the hindquarters through the gate, then back a few steps. When you have passed the end of the gate, push the hindquarters around left and guide the forehand until you are parallel to the gate. Side pass to close the gate.

You will also face the hinges of a left hand pull back through. Pull the gate toward the horse and side pass to the right. When your knee is past the end of the gate, guide the forehand around to the right and back through. Pivot to the right and side pass to the left to close and latch the gate.

Rope gates are often seen in trail classes. They are very easy to handle.

The "past the knee" requirement does not apply with rope gates. What you must do is make sure the horse's body is far enough through the gate before you make a turn to close the gate.

In competition, keep the movement slow and steady. In practice, slow way down, pausing and keeping the horse relaxed.

To increase the difficulty of working gates, place a pole along the bottom of the gate so the horse will have to step over when walking through. Never use a pole when backing through a gate.

Poles can also be set parallel to the gate about four feet from each side. Plants can be placed at the ends of the poles to entice the horse to nibble. Snacking is not allowed!

When working a gate, never take your hand from the gate.

Be very careful when working a rope gate that

the rope does not loop down and catch a stirrup. And don't let your horse attempt to chew the rope.

Reading a Course

Reading the course correctly is absolutely, positively required. Disqualification is the result if you go off course. You never know what is going to happen in a competition, with the exception of one thing: if you are disqualified, you are out.

Knowing that, you would be surprised at how many competitors get themselves disqualified simply because they didn't take the time to read the course.

Understand the written instructions. And be sure you follow the diagram. Both are posted at the arena, so there is no excuse for a failure here.

Make a mental note of the gate. Is it push, or pull, back through, right hand or left hand? Make a mental note of the turn arounds. How far do you turn around, and in what direction is the turn?

Now stand back and visualize yourself riding the course. Speaking out loud, tell a friend exactly how the course should be ridden.

Notice the last instruction on finishing the course. Does it say to jog out after the last obstacle? You are being judged on following all directions.

Always ask the course designer or the back gate person if any changes have been made to the course. It is your responsibility to know of any changes.

Walk the course. Find the correct path. Walk off the distances so you know the correct path. Say to yourself the places where you want to pick up the lope or break to the jog. Visualize your entire ride and see yourself riding smoothly through all transitions and obstacles.

Show Your Horse

If you are going to win trail classes, you must:

**Be prepared at the gate before the person showing ahead of you is finished with the course.

**Know your number and class designation.

**Be respectful and courteous to the judge.

Your goal in showing is to work the obstacles on a horse which is fluid and relaxed in his movement. So keep moving. Slow is fine, but try to avoid stopping and hesitating.

The most important thing to remember is you have a job, and your horse has a job. You are partners. Your job is to establish cadence and direct the horse on the correct path to the obstacle. Your horse's job is to work the obstacle. Let him do his job.

Mistakes are most often made when the rider decides to communicate with her horse while the horse is working an obstacle. The horse's attention is diverted from the obstacle to listen to the rider, and disaster! You ask, then you get out of the way. You must give the horse the freedom to be great.

Complete each obstacle before going to the next one. For example, jog completely out of the serpentine before picking up the lope. With an advanced western horse, what you think is what you get.

Suggested trail courses were designed by Quarter Horse trainer **Cherie Vonada**.

NOVICE COURSE

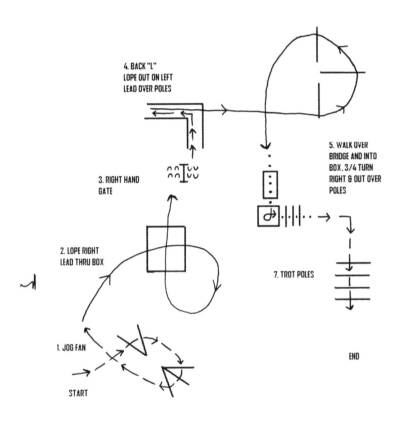

4. BACK "L"
LOPE OUT ON LEFT
LEAD OVER POLES

5. WALK OVER
BRIDGE AND INTO
BOX. 3/4 TURN
RIGHT & OUT OVER
POLES

3. RIGHT HAND
GATE

2. LOPE RIGHT
LEAD THRU BOX

7. TROT POLES

1. JOG FAN

END

START

ADVANCED COURSE

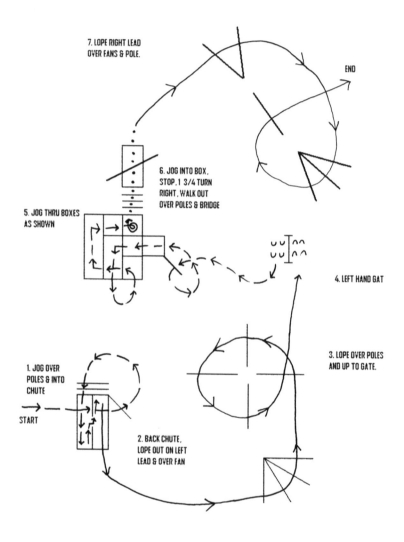

7. LOPE RIGHT LEAD OVER FANS & POLE.

END

6. JOG INTO BOX, STOP, 1 3/4 TURN RIGHT, WALK OUT OVER POLES & BRIDGE

5. JOG THRU BOXES AS SHOWN

4. LEFT HAND GAT

3. LOPE OVER POLES AND UP TO GATE.

1. JOG OVER POLES & INTO CHUTE

START

2. BACK CHUTE, LOPE OUT ON LEFT LEAD & OVER FAN

Training tip: Look up! As you take the first step in the class, remind yourself to look up. If you look down you will change your position and thereby change the horse's balance. The instant you start looking down, your score is going to go down.

Ride your horse at home as if you were at a show, and ride your horse at a show as if you were at home.

Don't change the communication system.

Don't try someone else's training techniques at the last minute. You and your horse can learn a new language later.

Right now say what you have always said, and mean what you have always meant.

You know your horse's capabilities. Trust him. Don't ask him for more, and he'll give you all he's got.

Finally, and most important of all, have fun, smile and enjoy the ride.

Cathy Hanson

Starting at age four, Cathy rode and showed western horses. At 17, she went to England to study dressage and jumping. She tested before the British Horse Society and earned her B.H.S.A.I. certificate before returning home to open a training stable.

Horses and riders trained by Cathy have won championships at western pleasure, western riding, trail, western horsemanship, showmanship, hunter under saddle, hunt seat equitation, hunter hack and working hunters.

A director of the Pacific Coast Quarter Horse Association since 1992, she has chaired the amateur and show committees as well as serving on the executive committee.

An active clinician, she was on the coaching team for the Youth World Cup. Her training and teaching techniques are featured in many magazines. She lives in San Juan Capistrano, CA.

Don Blazer

Whatever horsemen do with horses, Don has probably done. He isn't one to sit on fences just talking. He chooses to be part of the action.

He's trained and ridden everything from mustangs to Thoroughbreds, including western and English pleasure horses, reining horses, endurance racers and 300-yard sprinters. He's jumped horses, cut cattle, been over obstacles and around barrels.

He taught for five colleges, and he's traveled from Alaska to Australia demonstrating training techniques at seminars and workshops. He continues to do so as time permits.

He's the author of the syndicated column, A Horse, Of Course, which is must reading for thousands of fans. He's written "how-to" articles for most of the major equine publications.

He lives with his wife, Diane, in Scottsdale, AZ. They keep busy writing, riding and teaching.

Plain and simply, the information you want!

1. Make Money With Horses: The guide to profits with the breed you love. Choose weanlings, yearlings, broodmares or stallions. Start your own home-based business, and grow as the profits grow.

2. Nine Secrets of Perfect Horsemanship: Not about styles or disciplines, it's about how you can rev-up your riding and power-up your training. It's about thinking outside the box to benefit your horse.

3. Healthy Horses Seldom Burp!: The serious health-care book for the busy horse owner. Accurate, concise, packed with all the info you'll need to keep your horses happy and well for the next 20 years.

4. Walter Spills The Oats: Be the first to know, as Walter names names and tells it like it is--from a horse's point of view. Horse history, training tips, heroes and friends--straight from "the horse."

Success Is Easy books available at tack & book stores, or on the Internet at: **www.donblazer.com.** For catalog: Success Is Easy, 13610 N. Scottsdale, Suite 10-406, Scottsdale, AZ 85254